THE ART OF SPIRITUAL DIRECTION

A GUIDE TO IGNATIAN PRACTICE

Slightly adapted translation from
De kunst van geestelijke begeleiding,
Een praktijkboek in ignatiaans perspectief (2019)

JOS MOONS SJ

First published 2020 by Messenger Publications

English translation © Jos Moons SJ 2020

Originally published in Dutch as:
De kunst van geestelijke begeleiding. Een praktijkboek in ignatiaans perspectief
© 2019 Berne Media | abdij van berne, Heeswijk, The Netherlands
© 2019 Dr. Jos Moons SJ

The material in this publication is protected by copyright law. Except as may be permitted by law, no part of the material may be reproduced (including by storage in a retrieval system) or transmitted in any form or by any means, adapted, rented or lent without the written permission of the copyright owners. Applications for permissions should be addressed to the publisher.

The right of Jos Moons SJ to be identified as the author of the Work has been asserted by him in accordance with the Copyright and Related Rights Act, 2000.

ISBN 9781788121194
eISBN 9781788122573

Translated by Annie Bolger, Derrick Witherington, and Jos Moons,
with financial support from Tilburg School of Catholic Theology (Tilburg University),
a benefactor who wishes to remain anonymous, and the Society of Jesus.

Designed by Messenger Publications Design Department
Typeset in Adobe Caslon Pro and Bitter
Cover background image © Ekaterina Kamenetsky / Shutterstock.com
Printed by Hussar Books

Messenger Publications,
37 Leeson Place, Dublin D02 E5V0
www.messenger.ie

CONTENTS

Foreword: Paul Nicholson SJ 4

Introduction 7

1. A Guide to Ignatian Practice 10

2. Core Values: *An Ignatian Perspective on Spiritual Direction* 17

3. First Tool: *Taking It Easy* 39

4. Second Tool: *Listening by Following* 47

5. Third Tool: *Searching for Soul* 60

6. Fourth Tool: *Going Deeper* 76

7. Fifth Tool: *Evaluating* 101

8. Sixth Tool: *Forming for Spiritual Maturity* 122

9. Vocational Spiritual Direction 141

Conclusion 162

Word of Gratitude 165

Appendix 167

Bibliography 174

FOREWORD

It was Ignatius of Loyola himself who compared the methods of prayer and reflection that he was describing in his most famous writing, the *Spiritual Exercises*, to physical exercises: 'taking a walk, travelling on foot, and running'. One consequence of this is that the exercises need to be put into practice, not just outlined and analysed, if they are to have any effect. There is an exercise bike that stands in the corner of a room in the house where I live. It has unfortunately done little to promote the health of our Jesuit community, since no one has got onto it in the three years since it was given to us!

The Art of Spiritual Direction, the new book by Dutch Jesuit Dr Jos Moons SJ, clearly recognises this need to put theory into practice. It is true that it is rooted in a thorough study of the *Spiritual Exercises*, and the Ignatian tradition of spiritual direction that flows from them. But his desire in writing is less to analyse this tradition more deeply, and more to show how it can best be used in helping others to develop their relationship with God, and so come to know more clearly how God is calling them in the circumstances of their own lives.

Jos Moons speaks of two intended audiences for his book. First, it is offered to aspiring spiritual directors, offering them tools to use in their service of others through the process of spiritual accompaniment. Much of what is written here draws on training courses that he has offered in recent years. But it will also have value for those who have more experience in this field, sharing experiences of direction for them to compare with their own, and perhaps in that way putting words on approaches that they may have carried out in the past without too much reflection.

A particular feature of the book is its use of 'verbatims', transcribed conversations distilled from the author's experience in directing others and leading workshops. These are themselves an excellent teaching tool, inviting the reader to pause and ask 'What would I have said in response to that remark?', or 'Where do I think that this conversation if going?'. Experienced directors will develop their own style and approach. The point is not necessarily to parrot what the director in any particular verbatim would say, but to understand why they reacted in the way that they did, and thereby notice more clearly their own habitual patterns of response.

The work ends with a chapter on the accompaniment of vocational discernment. While it is important to be able to recognise the voice of God in life's everyday decisions, it is even more so in trying to choose which of many possible paths a whole life should follow. Here above all is where someone more ready to listen, and encourage the exploration of various possibilities without giving advice that shuts down options prematurely, is most needed. Ignatius was clear that ultimately it was God, not a spiritual director, who should point out to a person the path that they should follow. Jos Moons' work shows how that aspiration can be made a reality.

Readers may well be reminded of the ways in which Pope Francis has chosen to carry out his ministry since he was elected pope. His constant aim has been to help the Church and its members to become more discerning, to be able to listen to what the Spirit of God is saying in the midst of the clamour of other voices that surround us. Discernment is indeed an art, rather than an exact science. But, as with all arts, it can be improved by practice and by the guidance of other more experienced practitioners.

This book, then, is particularly timely, as the Church moves from government relying heavily on hierarchical authority to an outlook that draws more fully on the insights and opinions of all its members. If this process is to work well, those members must become skilled at reading 'the signs of the times' more accurately, attempting to recognise and put aside their own prejudices and knee-jerk reactions. A trained listener can be of immense help in enabling others to learn and practise this art of discernment, and what is written here can surely aid in the formation of such listeners. Whether as a resource for training courses, or a guide for those who find themselves called upon to accompany others, *The Art of Spiritual Direction* is to be warmly recommended.

Paul Nicholson SJ

Fr Paul Nicholson SJ, a British Jesuit, has served as director of Loyola Hall Spirituality Centre on Merseyside, and as novice-master of the North-West Europe Jesuit novitiate. He is currently Socius (i.e. assistant) to the provincial of the Jesuits in Britain, and is editor of The Way.

INTRODUCTION

This is a book about how to give spiritual direction. While several books on this topic have been published over the last twenty years or so, none of them focuses on concrete, clear and practical tools. It is this lacuna that I seek to fill with this book. You could even think of it as a manual.

Beginners in the art of spiritual accompaniment, whether ministers, priests or lay people, will learn in these pages a few 'tricks of the trade' that will help them to make this art their own. If you are a spiritual director with some experience, this book can provide vocabulary for your unconscious or unreflective practice; from now on you will knowingly and purposefully use certain tools while avoiding others. Additionally, the theoretical considerations in the book provide a theological and spiritual foundation for your acquired skills. Established spiritual directors may find it refreshing to hear familiar things explained by someone else.

The goal of this book is to help address a paradoxical need in the Church. On the one hand, spirituality is of the highest importance. The great twentieth-century Jesuit theologian Karl Rahner noted that the Christian of the future – whether Anglican, Calvinist, Catholic, Evangelical, Lutheran or Pentecostal – will only exist if he or she is a mystic. Rahner described what the faith of the future would look like and proposed that the most essential aspect would be a personal experience of God: 'The Christian of tomorrow will be a mystic'.[1] It is, indeed, precisely this experience that spiritual direction thematises, with the aim of quickening, deepening, and purifying it.

On the other hand, churches are in desperate need of good spiritual directors. I once had a Dutch seminary rector ask me, 'Where should I send my seminarians?' After I moved to Belgium, a bishop once asked me: 'To whom should I send young people who are searching for meaning? Or people who are discerning a vocation? Or those who are considering a career switch? Or those who cannot hear the voice of God?'

Furthermore, in a Roman Catholic context, this book is timely given the ecclesial culture that Pope Francis regularly promotes. This culture could be seen as not exclusively looking at the 'letter' of the law as expressed in the Catechism or in ecclesial rules, but as attempting to discern what is 'good' in a specific context and for concrete individuals. Spiritual direction is indispensable for this cultural shift.

The origin of this book lies in what I've learned as a Jesuit and from my experience as a Roman Catholic university chaplain and spiritual director in Amsterdam and Utrecht (The Netherlands) and Leuven (Belgium). In everything I have written here, I had in mind particular articles, spiritual directors, or courses. I recalled fragments of conversations and again was able to see particular names and faces. Missteps came to mind, as well as deep conversations that went very well. My specific background unavoidably shapes the style, examples, and ethos of this book, yet I hope that the book may be of service in other contexts than my Roman Catholic and Jesuit context. Here I think especially of our esteemed sisters and brothers from other Christian Churches.

---

[1] Here is Rahner's quote in context: 'The Christian of tomorrow will be a "mystic", one who has experienced something, or he or she will cease to be a Christian at all. For future Christian living will no longer be sustained and helped by the anonymous, manifest, and public convictions and religious customs of all, and that precede personal experience and decision. That means that the usual religious education as practiced hitherto can only provide a very secondary kind of preparation for the institutional elements in religion'. See 'Christian Living Today and Formerly', in *Theological Investigations*, vol. 7 (London: DLT), pp. 3–24, on p. 15. This is a substantially adapted translation on the basis of the original German, 'Frömmigkeit früher und heute' (1966).

Introduction

The book is assembled in the following manner. The opening chapters explain the foundation and mainly contain theoretical considerations. In the first chapter, I discuss a few other books written about spiritual direction and explain why I've chosen the format of a hands-on practical guide. The second chapter is devoted to offering some explanation of the framework out of which I work, namely, Ignatian spirituality. From the third chapter onwards, this book follows the format of 'a guide to Ignatian practice'. Each of these chapters introduces a particular tool, with ample illustrations of how one could concretely apply it in real spiritual accompaniment. I conclude by discussing a special case, namely, the direction of those discerning a vocation. After the conclusion follows a word of gratitude, for what does anyone have that he has not received from others?

Finally, spiritual accompaniment is not reserved for men. To designate spiritual directors and directees in this book, therefore, I will alternate between 'he' or 'his' and 'she' or 'her' and, less frequently, 'he or she'.

1.
A GUIDE TO IGNATIAN PRACTICE

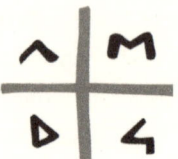

What sort of thing is spiritual direction? Is it a gift given from heaven, one that you may or may not possess? Is it something that comes with years of experience, something for wise old men and women? Or is it reserved for pastors, priests and religious? These examples all imply that spiritual accompaniment is something special, that some people have, and others do not. There is certainly such a thing as talent and aptitude. In biblical and theological language, we speak of spiritual gifts or so-called 'charisms' that are given to individual believers to serve and build up the Church and the world. In the Roman Catholic Church that notion was dusted off by the Second Vatican Council (see especially *Lumen Gentium*, no. 12). Yet by opting for 'a guide to Ignatian practice', this book points to a different, more accessible vision of spiritual direction. Spiritual direction is regarded here first and foremost as a craft, a practical skill in the most positive sense.

This interpretation is good news in that a skill can be learned, at least to some extent. That is the purpose of this book. I will present six concrete tools, which together form a kind of program. I'll give real examples in each chapter to show you how to use these tools. That means that the emphasis of this book is not on abstract reflections of a theological, spiritual, mystical or socio-psychological nature. A practical skill requires a practical approach, hence the subtitle 'A Guide to Ignatian Practice'.

My focus is unique in the sense that while a great deal has been written about spiritual direction, seldom do these books provide concrete tools. This applies, for example, to the acclaimed classic by fellow Jesuits William Barry and William Connolly, *The Practice of Spiritual Direction*.[2] Although their book contains helpful examples drawn from experience, including several pieces of dialogue, the emphasis is on theoretical considerations. The book is certainly very much worth reading; with great insight and clarity, the authors introduce an Ignatian vision of accompaniment. That is why I will, in the following chapters, refer to this book several times. That said, Barry and Connolly's book does not contain the concrete tools that the beginning spiritual director needs.

Also worth mentioning is the book for experienced spiritual directors written by the American Sister of Mercy Janet Ruffing, *Spiritual Direction: Beyond the Beginnings*.[3] She discusses important topics based on lots of experience and pays more attention than most authors to affective themes. For example, she talks about the importance of desire, about the tendency to resist experiences of intimacy with God and about guiding people in experiences of love and bridal mystery. But this book also does not introduce concrete tools.

The series of books on Ignatian spirituality and spiritual direction published at the beginning of this millennium by the acclaimed American Oblate of the Virgin Mary Timothy Gallagher are another case in point.[4] I admire Gallagher's practical approach; he develops his reflection with lots of examples from history, literature, biography and cases of actual spiritual direction. Unfortunately, his chosen cases of spiritual direction often have a 'high church' feel. This kind of scenario is typical: a woman tries to pray with the psalms and perseveres, despite

---

2   William Barry, William Connolly, *The Practice of Spiritual Direction*, 2nd rev. ed. (New York: Harper Collins, 2009), originally from 1982.
3   Janet Ruffing, *Spiritual Direction. Beyond the Beginnings* (New York: Paulist Press, 2000).
4   Timothy Gallagher, *The Discernments of Spirits. An Ignatian Guide for Everyday Living* (New York: Crossroad, 2005) and Timothy Gallagher, *Spiritual Consolation. An Ignatian Guide for Greater Discernment of Spirits* (New York: Crossroad, 2007). Together, these two books are a commentary on Ignatius of Loyola's two series of Rules for the Discernment of Spirits in the *Spiritual Exercises*. Gallagher also published books on the Examen Prayer and spiritual direction in the context of vocational discernment, see the bibliography at the end of this book.

distractions; then she comes across a verse that strongly appeals to her and assures her that God is with her in her struggles. While the example is comforting, it is my experience that God does not set entrance exams. It is my belief that God will concern himself with us even if we are not churchgoers, or pious or able to persevere; people with little faith practice may be touched by God very deeply. Moreover, this book does not discuss concrete tools either.

The *Beginner's Guide* that fellow Jesuit Richard Malloy published in 2017 may serve as a final example.[5] As the title suggests, it is very accessible. Malloy makes abundant use of anecdotes, examples and experiences (perhaps even too many!) and is in places highly entertaining. Yet, these can make the book look like a collection of wisdom, with the effect that spiritual direction can seem to consist in providing wisdom appropriate to the circumstances. Ironically, this is exactly the opposite of Malloy's vision of accompaniment, which is all about what is happening in the soul of the other person. My main objection, however, is that Malloy doesn't indicate what the spiritual director should actually do.

No Straitjacket

In short, I believe that there is a need in this field for something concrete and practical. *The Art of Spiritual Direction: An Ignatian Guide to Practice* is a useful addition to the existing body of literature on spiritual accompaniment. Nonetheless, it would be appropriate to make a few relativising remarks. A practical guide should not become a straitjacket. Similarly to the great dogmas of faith that are meant to point the way to the faith but are not themselves *the faith*, the tools presented in this book are meant to point the way, not to be stringently applied.

Moreover, while I unfold in this book how spiritual accompaniment works step-by-step, actual spiritual conversations rarely develop in a linear way. Additionally, tools are not the only necessity for effective spiritual direction; spiritual directors also need certain human qualities, life experiences and attitudes. Without personal warmth, self-confidence, affective freedom, familiarity with the spiritual realm and

---

[5] Richard G. Malloy, *Spiritual Direction. A Beginner's Guide* (Maryknoll: Orbis, 2017).

some experience of personal crises, the tools presented here are useless.[6]

Another important observation to put things into perspective is that this book promotes only one possible model of spiritual accompaniment. It is based on certain Christian convictions, which could be traded for other Christian convictions. My proposal is not the only door to accompaniment. Think for example of other spiritual families with a tradition of spiritual accompaniment, such as the Benedictines or Carmelites or, more recently, the charismatic family. Even within these traditions there exists a certain plurality; different practitioners accentuate different things. Moreover, in what follows I usually present a way of reacting that has proven helpful in my Ignatian practice, while in reality multiple reactions are often possible and correct. Sometimes I mention other possibilities, sometimes I don't. If I simplify, I do so for pedagogical reasons.

Target Audience

With these limitations, this book can be useful for those who are finding their feet in the art of spiritual direction. To learn, it is usually best to follow instructions for a while. Students of spiritual direction should not say too quickly that they have their own way of doing things; they should first learn the art. When I learned to ride a horse, it didn't make much sense to be stubborn and to persist in my way of doing things; after all, I was learning something I didn't know much about. If you're baking an apple pie for the first time, it's best simply to follow the recipe. After you learn the recipe, you can customise and follow your own ideas. You then do so 'hindered' by knowledge and experience.

Yet, this book can also be useful for those who have experience and want to revisit or reconsider that experience. It can be a critical mirror confirming or questioning existing practice. It doesn't say how it should be done, but how it can be done. If you do certain things differently yourself, can you explain why you do so? And what is the advantage of your own approach?

---

6 For a more extensive treatment of these human qualities, life experiences, and attitudes, see the insightful chapter 'Becoming a Spiritual Director', in Barry, Connolly, *The Practice of Spiritual Direction*, pp. 127–141.

Further, this book is useful for complicated cases, when you cannot rely on spontaneous intuition, for example in the case of people who are traumatised. This book offers you the basics, which you can then rely on in those instances. When I drove for the first time in England, that is, 'on the wrong side of the road', I returned to what my driving instructor had told me. 'Inside mirror – outside mirror – shoulder'. Normally, you do these things spontaneously; in another context, you have to deliberately follow the procedure.

Affective Orthodoxy

Thus, this book aims above all to be a hands-on, practical guide that focuses on developing practical skills. Still, much is at stake in that seemingly simple agenda. This book thematises the neglected topic of interiority.

As far as the Roman Catholic Church is concerned, for example, much attention is paid to the *content of faith*. This often has a liturgical and moral expression: we tend to observe rules and regulations, sometimes down to the smallest details. Hopefully, there will also be attention to the *life of faith*, to Christian charity and 'orthopraxis'. In concrete terms, a Eucharistic celebration will not only make use of the correct liturgical texts or feature a proper sermon but will go hand-in-hand with a real commitment to our brothers and sisters. 'Show me your faith through your deeds', as we read in Scripture.

But that is not enough. The Church should also pay attention to the soul and to interiority. After all, the Christian life is not only about doctrine and practice, but also about spirituality. What about the alternation in the soul between warm and cold, love and hate, mildness and hardness, devotion and faithfulness, and hopelessness and unbelief? What do these inner movements have to say? Which ones have to do with God, and which ones do not? How does one deal with this inner world? I feel that too little attention is paid to this realm of interiority, spirituality and the soul, and that's a shame.[7]

---

7 Cf. Benedictine abbot André Louf's warning for an 'excessive rationalisation of morality' and his plea for what such legalism forgets, the deeper reality of the heart and its (spiritual) desires. The following quote is instructive: 'It is not as important to know if the decision will conform to a rule laid down by moralists, but rather to have the concre experience of the Spirit's leading at the core of some decision. From that moment, the real question is of this order: what is the real nature

To put it plainly, one cannot be a Christian without paying heed to God's voice speaking inwardly. These last words are not my words; in *Gaudium et Spes* (the Pastoral Constitution on the Church in the Modern World), one of the four constitutions that resulted from the Second Vatican Council, it is written that 'Conscience is the most intimate center and sanctuary of a person, in which he or she is alone with God whose voice echoes within them' (GS, 16).[8] It is not sufficient, therefore, to stick to the Church's doctrinal or moral teachings. Church leaders have the task 'to form consciences, not to replace them', as Pope Francis declared in his encyclical *Amoris Laetitia* (The Joy of Love).[9]

In order to form consciences, it is necessary to know the movements in the soul, their multiplicity, their beauty and their deceptiveness. The Christian is inhabited and moved by spirits (figuratively speaking) of peace, joy, goodness, patience – the Holy Spirit. But equally moved by spirits of cold duty, angry frustration for the shortcomings of others, or cynicism (for example, cynicism about society, or the bishop, or other leaders). To return to the example of a Eucharistic celebration: it requires not only the right content, texts, and charity, but also the right inner movements and spirituality. I have the impression that the same applies to other Christian Churches.

Yet tragically, in ecclesiastical contexts, spirituality and interiority sometimes seem to be viewed as a threat. That fear may be caused by mottos such as 'believing without belonging' or 'spirituality yes, Church no' and the popularity of magazines and programs promoting superficial 'feel good' spirituality. In this book I do not consider the popularity of spirituality as a threat to the Churches, but as a critical mirror that compels us to question whether in our zeal for orthodoxy and orthopraxy, we may be forgetting something? Have we forgotten the soul, interiority, spirituality?

---

of the desire by which I am being led – insofar as such a discernment is possible – and to what extent can this desire be concretely assumed by the impulse of the Holy Spirit within my soul'. See *Grace Can Do More. Spiritual Accompaniment and Spiritual Growth* (Kalamazoo: Cistercian Publications, 2002), pp. 7–12, quote on p. 9; originally in French, *La grace peut advantage. L'accompagnement spirituel* (1992).

8   Texts from the Second Vatican Council will be quoted in the translation published in *Decrees of the Ecumenical Councils*, ed. Norman Tanner (Washington: Georgetown University Press, 1990).
9   Pope Francis, *Amoris Laetitia. Post-Synodal Apostolic Exhortation on Love in the Family* (Vatican: Vatican Press, 2016), no. 37. Available online at vatican.va.

In short, the indirect agenda of this book is to put interiority on the agenda. I want to contribute to making more room in ecclesiastical life for what I call 'affective orthodoxy' for lack of a better word.[10] In a certain sense, this book goes with the flow of the popularity of spirituality, albeit, as we shall see, not uncritically. One of the key insights from and for the world of the soul and interiority is that anything can be deceptive; not everything that glitters is gold.

Promise

Finally, learning the craft of spiritual direction is hard work. But the worker deserves his wage; this book carries a promise. Those who accompany others well are rewarded – the Germans say 'gifted' (*beschenkt*) – with the gift of being a witness of what they have helped to awaken: the inner experience of a God who loves each human person.

---

[10] I wrote about this in a (Dutch language) column 'Affectieve orthodoxie' (www.igniswebmagazine.nl, 2-2-2015) in which I contend that for a proper Christian life, doctrine (orthodoxy) and practise (orthopraxis) are not sufficient; it is also about a purified interiority and discernment of spirits.

2. CORE VALUES

AN IGNATIAN PERSPECTIVE ON SPIRITUAL DIRECTION

Let us suppose that you talk to Anne, a middle-aged Trappistine sister, who's going through a bit of a crisis.[11] To her dismay, she sometimes thinks about leaving the monastery. Her abbess has sent her to you. Anne tells about her life as a Trappistine sister: about her fellow sisters, especially the abbess, with whom she has a good relationship, about her journey so far and about the current situation. Finally, she asks if you can help her. What would you do?

Now this example might feel alienating. You may have no clue about what a Trappist is, except that you've heard of Trappist beer! Or maybe you wonder why we would work with such a negative example? For the purpose of the book, the details of the cases do not matter much. After each example, you should add 'or something like this'. If that makes it more relevant or credible for you, change this case into a student who wants to change her major, a husband who falls in love with another woman, a banker with a midlife crisis, etc. Or just stay with Anne, the Trappistine sister.

Of course, the spiritual director who you are does not immediately solve Anne's crisis by answering the concrete question at the end of her story. You first need to find out more about Anne, her crisis and her soul. But what exactly will you ask? In what direction should you guide

---

11   The cases in this book have been invented, unavoidably my imagination is marked by my experience over the past years.

this conversation? And for what purpose? Do you intend to give some advice later on or not? And if so, what then do you aim for?

All the choices you make during your conversation depend on implicit spiritual and theological convictions that together form some sort of a theoretical framework. In other words, even if spiritual direction is a practical skill, it presupposes theory. Just like a carpenter cannot exert his practical skill without the theoretical framework of mathematics and mechanics, which form the basis of it. In the same way, a spiritual director always has a theoretical framework, consisting not of mathematics and mechanics, but of convictions of a spiritual and theological nature. In this chapter I discuss that framework by highlighting four core values: the director's restraint, which demonstrates respect for the directee; the importance of spiritual experience, the preference for what leads to life and the formation towards spiritual maturity. In doing so, I draw from the source of Ignatian spirituality.

(1) Reverence and Restraint

The first core value is respect for the directee. Everyday experiences with colleagues, housemates or family amply provide us with evidence that the other is really different. The French eloquently call this the otherness of the other person, *l'altérité de l'autre*. We must respect that otherness.

One could also think of the beautiful reflections of the Jewish philosopher Martin Buber in his book *I and Thou*.[12] He wonders about how we respond to what we encounter around us: other people, animals, things. According to Buber, there are essentially two attitudes or ways of perceiving and reacting. The first perceives the outside world as 'it' (*Es*) and treats things and people as objects or things. This applies not only to people but to everything: trees, food, art, pets, etc. The second attitude or way of perceiving and responding is essentially about a relationship, in which what was once perceived as just a thing is recognised as a 'Thou' (*Du*). The shift is a shift from objectification to reverence. What I encounter is beyond my categories such that I should not try to understand or control or use it; rather, I should welcome the relationship

---

12 Martin Buber, *I and Thou*, tr. R.G. Smith (Edinburgh: Clark, 1984); originally in German, *Ich und Du* (1923).

I find myself in and marvel in surprise. I understand Buber's reflection, which is as sharp and confrontational as it is warm and inspiring, as a plea for reverent attention.

However, the respect of the spiritual director for the directee goes deeper than our daily experiences of the other person's otherness, even if deepened with spiritual-philosophical reflections such as those of Buber. It is rooted in the faith conviction that God interacts with each human being personally.

This idea that God relates personally to each person features prominently in the introductory notes at the beginning of the *Spiritual Exercises**. (Words with an asterisk are explained in the appendix.) The *Spiritual Exercises* is a booklet written by Ignatius of Loyola* (1491–1556), the driving force behind a small group of friends who founded the Society of Jesus, commonly known as the Jesuits*. The booklet contains recommendations on how to give a retreat and what content to offer to the retreatant. It is meant for those who accompany others on a retreat, not for the retreatant. In one of the introductory comments, Ignatius admonished the spiritual director to restrain himself. He explains this as follows:

> It is more appropriate and far better that the Creator and Lord himself should communicate himself to the devout soul embracing it in love and praise, and disposing it for the way which will enable the soul to serve him better in the future. Accordingly, the one giving the Exercises ought not to lean or incline in either direction but rather, while standing by like the pointer of a scale in the equilibrium, to allow the Creator to deal immediately with the creature and the creature with its Creator and Lord.[13]

---

13 The *Spiritual Exercises of Saint Ignatius. A Translation and Commentary by George E. Ganss* (St. Louis: The Institute of Jesuit Sources, 1992), no. 15. Cf. the invitation to the so-called colloquy, that is, an intimate conversation 'in the way one friend speaks to another, or a servant to one in authority – now begging a favour, now accusing oneself of some misdeed, now telling one's concerns and asking for counsel about them', the *Spiritual Exercises*, no. 54; this type of conversation is recommended as the conclusion to each prayer time, see the *Spiritual Exercises*, e.g. nos. 61, 62, 63, 64, 71.

Thus, the spiritual director should be very careful not to make suggestions and proposals regarding possible decisions about the future; the director should instead 'allow the Creator to deal immediately with the creature and the creature with its Creator and Lord'. This exhortation rests on a deep theological and spiritual foundation. It is rooted in the conviction that God himself interacts with each and every human person. It bears witness to a great confidence in that direct, unmediated relationship.[14]

Therefore, from an Ignatian perspective, it is perhaps better to speak of spiritual accompaniment than spiritual direction, and to call the spiritual director a 'spiritual companion'. If it is indeed God himself who interacts with the human person, then God, in intimate dialogue with the person, is the director. Here the sharp warning from the Gospel has lost nothing of its relevance: 'But you are not to be called rabbi, for you have one teacher, and you are all students. And call no one your father on earth, for you have one Father – the one in heaven. Nor are you to be called instructors, for you have one instructor, the Messiah' (Mt 23:8–10, NRSV). In what follows, I frequently follow common usage of the words *direction*, *director* and *directee*, but I alternate these with the theologically and spiritually more fitting terms *accompaniment*, *companion* and *accompanied person*.[15]

The sensitivity for God as the ultimate director is not unique to the Jesuits. The Trappist monk and spiritual writer André Louf has the same preference.[16] According to another Trappist monk, Bernardo Olivera, the Spirit plays the most important role in direction. Quoting John of the Cross, Olivera warns that there is only one guide:

---

14 Anyone interested in reading more about this will find delight in Karl Rahner's compelling fictitious letter from Ignatius, published as *Ignatius of Loyola Speaks*, tr. Annemarie S. Kidder (South Bend, IN: St. Augustine's Press, 2013); originally 'Das Alte neu sagen. Eine fiktive Rede des Ignatius von Loyola an einen Jesuiten von heute' (1978).
15 To my surprise, Barry and Connolly prefer the term direction. They explain: '"Direction" does suggest something more than advice-giving and problem-solving. It implies that the person who seeks direction is going somewhere and wants to talk to someone on the way. It implies, too, that the talk will not be casual and aimless, but apt to help the person find a way'. See *The Practice of Spiritual Direction*, pp. 9–11, quote on p. 11. Their reasoning is not entirely convincing, as these arguments apply to spiritual accompaniment as well.
16 See Louf, *Grace Can Do More*, pp. 42–44.

Directors should reflect that they themselves are not the chief agent, guide, and mover of souls in this matter, but that the principal guide is the Holy Spirit, who is never neglectful of souls.[17]

As an aside, it is worthwhile to note that Olivera speaks emphatically about spiritual motherhood as well as fatherhood, a concept from the tradition of the Desert Fathers and Mothers. (From the late second century onwards, Christians went to the desert in search of God, especially around Scetis – modern day Wadi El Natrun – in northern Egypt. Acknowledging the need for spiritual accompaniment, they recognised the gift of wisdom that some of them had. Because of their spiritual leadership, these wise hermits came to be called the Desert Fathers and Mothers.) The motherly and fatherly role that Olivera thematises implies that spiritual companions do have an important role. Next to, with, and under the Spirit, they are fathers and mothers.[18]

Basically, this first core value boils down to asceticism. The interest of the spiritual director should be given radically to what happens in the soul of the other person. How does God communicate with her or him? How things work in the director's own soul is barely relevant. It is about the Creator and the other creature, not about the director. To make this more personal, let's return to the case at the beginning of this chapter: it's about Anne and her experiences and questions, not about my experiences, questions, or insights. In the chapters to come we will see what this attitude of reverence and asceticism looks like in concrete terms.

---

17 Bernardo Olivera, *Light for My Path. Spiritual Accompaniment* (Collegeville, MN: Liturgical Press, 2009), p. 1; originally *Luz para mi pasos: iniciación al acompañamiento spiritual en el context monástico* (2004). The quote continues by specifying that the spiritual companion has a mediating role: 'and that they are instruments for directing them to perfection through faith and the law of God, according to the spirit God gives each one'.
18 See Olivera, *Light for My Path. Spiritual Accompaniment*, pp. 9–17. According to Olivera, each 'guide' or 'accompanist' – the choice of words is somewhat odd – ideally represents both motherly and fatherly parenthood. This is a valuable perspective that deserves attention in our generally male-oriented Christian Churches.

(2) Spiritual Experience

Essential for spiritual accompaniment, moreover, is the directee's spiritual experience.[19] In their standard work on spiritual direction, Jesuits Barry and Connolly place great emphasis on this. They make the comparison with cooking and then claim:

> Religious experience is to spiritual direction what foodstuff is to cooking. Without foodstuff there can be no cooking. Without religious experience there can be no spiritual direction.[20]

As Barry and Connolly point out, this element of experience can be found in various forms and shapes, both in the mysticism of all times and amongst renowned theologians such as Karl Rahner and Bernard Lonergan.[21] In this book, reflection on experience is traced back to Ignatius in particular. A typical Basque, he was a fiery man full of passion with a rich inner world. Gradually, Ignatius noticed that God had something to say to him through what he experienced within himself. He did not have to deny his feeling and passion; on the contrary, he had to befriend his experience and learn to find his way in it.

For example, Ignatius recounts how he was hit by a cannonball during an overconfident defense of a city – we are in the sixteenth century – and ended up on a sickbed. There he surrendered himself to daydreaming about the world of chivalry, castles, damsels, and victory, which he alternated with reveries about following Christ. Both kinds of fantasies were enchanting, but the first kind quickly withered, while the second retained its salutary taste. Increasingly, Ignatius understood that

---

19 What follows here repeats some ideas that were published as Jos Moons, 'Pleidooi voor een alternatieve strategie bij pastorale dilemma's. «Dat wij zouden aanvoelen wat Gods meest heilige wil is, en hem volbrengen» (Ignatius)', in *Internationaal Katholiek Tijdschrift Communio* 42 (2017), 479–488.
20 Barry, Connolly, *The Practice of Spiritual Direction*, p. 8; one could stretch the word spiritual to include all inner experience.
21 For a more elaborate treatment of this, see Barry, Connolly, *The Practice of Spiritual Direction*, second chapter, 'The Centrality of Religious Dimension of Experience', pp. 13–28. Janet Ruffing's plea to explore one's desires is based on similar convictions, see *Spiritual Direction*, first chapter, pp. 9–31.

God wanted to say something to him through that difference.[22] It was not the content of the dream that mattered, but the affective 'aftertaste'; Ignatius learned that God speaks by means of the affective effect in the soul. To be able to discern God's presence, however, he first had to enter into contact with his inner being. Without foodstuff, there can be no cooking.

The example also clarifies what spiritual experience is. It is less about the content of what you consider, do or think and more about what resonates within: the aftertaste, the experience, the color or atmosphere. What are these and how do they develop? That is what we call spiritual experience. In this understanding, experience does not have to be spectacular; usually it is very ordinary. In the example of Ignatius' daydreams, there are no flashes of lightning and there is no loud voice, no grand sign in the sky, no magnificent miracle. Instead it is about a subtle inner experience that one easily fails to notice.

Let us see how that may work with Anne, whom we met at the beginning of this chapter. It could be that she has been very unhappy lately. She feels lonely and notices that her heart has been growing cold: she speaks bitterly about her fellow sisters. Or perhaps the situation is very different. She may be in a positive flow: she is looking for a new challenge, a new sense of direction in a life outside the walls of the monastery. It could be that this is very clear to her and that she feels relieved at the thought of starting all over again. No matter which scenario is correct, these are all examples of spiritual experience.

This kind of spiritual experience exists in many other forms. It can be about experiencing strength, mildness, simplicity, clarity, light, trust, depth, connectedness, warmth, wisdom. Ignatius mentions as examples of this kind of experience 'courage and strength, consolations, tears, inspirations, and tranquility', that everything is easy, that you grow in love for God, faith, hope, love and peace in God. A good example from

---

22 See 'Reminiscences or Autobiography of Ignatius Loyola, as heard and written down by Luis Gonçalves Da Câmara', in *Personal Writings. Reminiscences, Spiritual Diary, Select Letters, Including the Text of the Spiritual Exercises*, tr. and intr. J.A. Munitiz and Ph. Endean (London: Penguin Books, 1996), pp. 3–64, nos. 1–8. Also called 'A Pilgrim's Journey', this is a well-constructed narration for the edification of others, probably novices, rather than a historically accurate autobiography. By outlining the process of his own spiritual refinement, with God acting as his 'schoolteacher' (no. 27), Ignatius hoped to stimulate a similar growth in others.

the Bible is the enumeration in Paul's letter to the Galatians of what he calls the fruits of the Spirit:

> Love, joy, peace, patience, kindness, generosity, faithfulness, gentleness and self-control. (Gal 5:22, NRSV)

Your experience can also be very different and include anxiety, cynicism, lethargy, being closed, hardness, coldness, insecurity, superficiality, feeling blocked. Ignatius mentions, among other things, 'obtuseness of soul, turmoil within it, an impulsive motion toward low and earthly things, or disquiet from various agitations and temptations', the experience of confusion, sadness, delusion, unrest, despair, absence of hope and love, laziness, feeling lukewarm, and feeling separated from God.[23]

Hermeneutics
What is the theoretical framework of this preference for experience? According to Ignatius's experience and conviction, the affective-spiritual domain is an important *locus* or site to find God. God communicates with us through what we experience, feel, and sense. A recent dictionary of Ignatian spirituality explains that the Spanish word *sentir* (feel), is indeed 'one of the most characteristic terms in Ignatian anthropology and spirituality'.[24] The Creator who interacts immediately with the creature does this by way of the human person's inner movements.

Ignatian spirituality approaches these diverse experiences with a very distinct hermeneutic (that it shares with other traditions) by distinguishing between two basic categories. Focusing on inner aftertaste, it seeks to assess whether or not the inner experience leads to an increase in the relationship with the self, God, others and the Kingdom, or not. For example, on the one hand, one has the spiritual

---

23 *Spiritual Exercises*, nos. 315, 316, 317.
24 Javier Melloni, 'Sentir', in *Diccionario de Espiritualidad Ignaciana*, eds. J. Melloni a.o. (Bilbao – Santander: Mensajero, 2007), pp. 1631–1637, on p. 1631. Cf. the lemma's opening sentences: '*Estamos ante uno de los términos más característicos de la antropología y espiritualidad ignacianas. En el sentir están concentrados muchos componentes psíquicos y espirituales implicados en la experiencia de Dios vivida por S. Ignatio y propuesta por él*'.

experience of a beautiful Easter vigil or a silent prayer in a church, mild thoughts about the faults of others, devotion to the Kingdom in the form of active charity or generosity, intellectual simplicity and clarity, thankfulness and wonder. This category Ignatius calls *consolation*; it stimulates an increase in faith, hope, love. On the other hand, one could think of reluctance to pray, impatience with fellow human beings, superficial concern for oneself, intellectual confusion, cynicism. Ignatius terms that category *desolation*; it hinders an increase in faith, hope, love.[25]

Radical

Ignatius's many letters illustrate how radical this preference for experience is. After giving his instructions, often in detailed form and not without some force, Ignatius frequently concluded with a farewell wish to sense God's will and act accordingly. (It is helpful to note that what Ignatius refers to as 'God's will' is akin to *where God is to be found* or *that which is most beneficial*. The idea that God has a blueprint for everything and that in that sense there exists a will of God which we must carry out, implies undesirable concepts of humankind as well as of God.) For example, Ignatius once sent a letter to the Jesuits in Gandía (Spain) full of instructions and teachings on obedience which he concluded with these words:

> By his infinite and supreme goodness may he deign to give us his perfect grace, so that we may feel [or sense] his holy will and entirely fulfil it.[26]

---

[25] Much more could be said about this, amongst others that consolation can be deceiving and in fact be desolation. Therefore, the English Jesuit Rob Marsh prefers the terms movement and counter-movement: something that goes in the direction of salvation and God or in the opposite direction. See for example Robert Marsh, 'Receiving and Rejecting. On Finding a Way in Spiritual Direction', in *The Way. A Review of Christian Spirituality Published by the British Jesuits* 45/1 (2006), pp. 7–21

[26] *Letters and Instructions*, ed. and tr. M. Palmer, J. Padberg and J. McCarthy (St. Louis: The Institute of Jesuit Sources, 2006), p. 201; letter dated 29 July 1547. I have replaced 'know' with 'feel (or sense)', on the basis of the Spanish original, which reads *sentir*: '*Quien por su infinita y summa bondad nos quiera dar su gratia cumplida para que su santíssima voluntad sintamos, y aquella enteramente cumplamos*', *Monumenta Historica Societatis Iesu* (MHSI), *Monumenta Ignatiana Series Prima*, vol. I, p. 562.

In other words, what mattered ultimately were not Ignatius's insights and instructions but rather the inner experience of the Jesuits themselves, for example, in the form of spiritual joy and communion with God or a keen sense of what was beneficial and what would best serve God.

Non-Jesuits too were advised to feel God's will. Ignatius concluded an extensive letter on spirituality to the Spanish Benedictine sister Teresa de Rajadell as follows: 'I end by praying the most Holy Trinity to give us, through their infinite and supreme goodness, the fullness of grace, so that we may feel their most holy will and fulfil it completely'.[27] Writing to the Viceroy of Sicily Juan de Vega, he concluded with the following greeting: 'to Your Lordship (…) may he deign to grant his abundant grace, so that we may always feel (or sense) his most holy will and perfectly fulfill it'.[28]

This conviction that spiritual experience is a reliable source of orientation is easily neglected, forgotten, or treated with suspicion. Worthwhile for promoting this conviction and demonstrating its solid roots are the bestselling books by the English Jesuit Gerhard Hughes, *God of Surprises* (1985) and by the German Benedictine monks Anselm Grün and Meinrad Dufner, *Spiritualität von Unten* or 'Spirituality from Below' (1996).[29] Gerhard Hughes uses, among other things, the image of riding a wild horse. We tend to want to gain control of the bucking horse; but does the horse's caprice have something to say to us?[30] The horse represents our inner life, our soul. Hughes makes the case that these diverse experiences in our souls – the ups and downs, the happiness and confusion – have much to say to us about God.

---

[27] See *Personal Writings*, pp. 134–135; letter dated June 18, 1536. Here too, *Letters and Instructions* unfortunately translates 'know': 'I close, praying that the Most Holy Trinity by its infinite and supreme goodness may bestow upon all of us abundant grace, so that we may know its most holy will and entirely fulfil it', on p. 22. Cf. however the Spanish original: '*para que su santísima santa voluntad sintamos, y aquella enteramente la cumplamos*', MHSI, *Monumenta Ignatiana*, vol. I, p. 107.

[28] *Letters and Instructions*, p. 307; letter dated April 12, 1550. Once again, I have changed 'know' into 'feel (or sense)' on the basis of the Spanish original, see MHSI, *Monumenta Ignatiana*, vol. III, p. 15: '*para que su santísima voluntad siempre sintamos*'.

[29] Gerhard W. Hughes, *God of Surprises* (London: DLT, 1985); it saw various reprints and was translated into more than twenty languages, amongst which Dutch, *Een God van verrassingen* (1996), and Spanish, *El Dios de las sorpresas* (2012). Anselm Grün and Meinrad Dufner, *Spiritualität von Unten* (Münsterschwarzach: Vier Türme Verlag, 1994); it saw various reprints and was translated into various languages, including Spanish, *Una espiritualidad desde abajo. El diálogo con Dios desde el fondo de la persona* (2000); there is no English translation.

[30] See Hughes, *God of Surprises*, pp. 6–7.

The Benedictine monks Grün and Dufner argue on the basis of the monastic tradition for a Christian spirituality that not only strives for the ideal, but also seeks and finds orientation – and indeed God – in experiences of failure, limitation, shortcomings, and sin, for these open us up to true humility. Although the latter book does not discuss discernment, which is essential for a reliable spirituality from below, it is valuable for considering 'unfashionable' experiences to be a constructive part of the journey of faith. Moreover, it confirms my point that there is a broad tradition of interiority, which in the case of the monastic tradition particularly takes the form of humility.

Attention to Inner Movements
The anthropological and theological assumptions about God's direct communication through our inner movements that I elaborated above lead us to a second core value for spiritual accompaniment: it should focus on spiritual experience. It is about God at the level of inner movements. In St Beunos, the Jesuit Spirituality Centre in North Wales, this vision of accompaniment has been translated into a kind of program. According to this program, spiritual accompaniment consists of three steps:

    Listen,

    notice,

    stay.

The spiritual director's task is in the first place to *listen*. While doing so, he or she is on the lookout for inner movements, for where the waters are moving, for spiritual experiences that should be noticed. Finally, the spiritual director should invite the directee to stay with those experiences and deepen them in the rest of the conversation. The interest in spiritual experience means that it is much less about other things: 'So the focus is not problem solving, catechesis, theological reflection, or teaching what spirituality is', writes Ruth Holgate, who for many years trained spiritual directors.[31]

---

31 Ruth Holgate, 'Training Spiritual Directors', in *The Way. A Review of Christian Spirituality Published by the British Jesuits* 53/4 (2014), pp. 68–78, on p. 72.

Let's go back to Anne. The primary task of her spiritual companion is not to teach Church doctrine by reminding her of the value of faithfulness and encouraging her to be faithful to her 'yes'. The companion's main concern should neither be to comfort by affirming that it is indeed difficult, nor to give practical advice on how best to solve this. No, first and foremost, the spiritual companion should explore what Anne is experiencing.

This cannot be done without also asking what Anne thinks and what she does. And it is probably good to let Anne know that you sympathise with her difficult situation. But your ultimate interest is what is happening in her soul. As soon as it is possible you should leave the layer of the narrative and the events and begin a conversation at the layer of experience. When Anne complains that she rarely has good conversations with fellow sisters or that the monastery lacks human warmth, your interest should not be in the details of how bad her housemates are but in the details of her experience. What is it like to experience that loneliness? Can she describe what kind of loneliness it is? What kind of bitterness? Does she experience bitterness more generally, perhaps? How does she respond to the bitterness that wells up in her? And is that all there is? In other words: is it only dark and heavy, or is there also light? And if there is also light, can we talk about that for a moment? In short, anything the directee says is of course welcome, but the spiritual director is mainly interested in what is bubbling beneath the surface of the events and narratives.

It is clear that here too asceticism plays an important role. The spiritual director may be interested to know exactly what is going on. He may be indignant about Anne's fellow sisters or concerned about the value of Anne's 'yes'. However, all these things should hardly matter for good spiritual directors: one's own theological position, personal indignation, concern for this or that, must be set aside to give space for the directee. What matters principally is the directee and his or her spiritual experience.[32]

---

[32] Barry and Connolly make a similar plea, using the example of a married woman who is in love with somebody else. They state that the spiritual director's role is to stand with the woman, to talk with her about prayer and about her relationship with God, arguing that 'conflicting loyalties tend to interfere with the director's ability to listen'. Insofar as you are worried, you could translate that

(3) Privileging What Leads to Life

Spiritual accompaniment is about what is bubbling up in the soul. But within the wide and varied realm of the soul, not everything is equally significant. Not all experiences deserve the same attention. We should privilege those experiences that have to do with God or with the Kingdom and that are beneficial. The third core value of Ignatian spiritual direction consists in this preference for what leads to life.

That sounds clear and self-evident. Surely it is obvious that we speak more about salvation, and less about doom? And yet it is not so. The English Jesuit Robert Marsh explains in a sublime essay on spiritual direction that directors suffer from a 'therapeutic seduction'.[33] Spiritual directors tend to want to talk about what goes wrong, about problems, about pitfalls, in order to heroically save their directee from those perils. As a doctor of souls, he focuses on illness, trying to bring healing, like a therapist wearing a Christian spiritual hat. This therapeutic temptation puts on decent – even praiseworthy! – disguises, such as the fight against evil, injustice, and sin. Isn't correcting injustice and purifying sin a wonderful task? Doesn't the reality of evil mean that we have to take it seriously by paying attention to it? Shouldn't we confront people with themselves, with the Gospel, with others, so that they may repent, as Olivera states?[34]

In Ignatian spiritual accompaniment, however, confrontation only has a modest place and therapeutic seduction is to be avoided. The reason for this is not that qualified psychologists are better therapists (which they usually are) nor that evil does not exist as a real threat (which it is). The reason is simply that God is always present and that he always works. For example, at the end of the Ignatian thirty-day retreat, the retreatant contemplates

---

into questions, e.g. on how the God she longs for looks on her, or how she reconciles her behavior with Christian values. See Barry, Connolly, *The Practice of Spiritual Direction*, pp. 150–152.

33 Thus one of the headings in Marsh, 'Receiving and Rejecting. On Finding a Way in Spiritual Direction', see pp. 13–15.

34 Olivera considers this one of the three essential tasks or functions of the spiritual director, see Olivera, *Light for My Path*, p. 54; he elaborates this confrontation in relation to personal life, the gospel, monastic life and community life, see pp. 54–59.

how God labours and works for me in all the creatures on the face of the earth;
that is, he acts in the manner of one who is labouring.
For example, he is working in the heavens, elements, plants, fruits, cattle, and all the rest – giving them their existence, conserving them, concurring with their vegetative and sensitive activities, and so forth.[35]

For sure this labouring, toiling God is stronger than evil. Therefore, your main interest should be in what God is doing and how God is present. Essentially spiritual accompaniment is about the soul and about God, and in more implicit terms, also about what is good, beneficial, alive and life-giving.

It goes without saying that once again asceticism is important. Ironically, our natural tendency is sometimes to delve into where God is absent and where there is death and darkness rather than life and light. We must forcefully resist that tendency.

You may already sense that a second difficulty immediately arises. How do you know what is life-giving and what is not? How do you privilege what is good? It is not always clear what has to do with God and what does not. It is as serious a misconception to think that everything that is pleasant, fine, and gentle has to do with God, as it is to think that what is complicated, difficult, and heavy cannot be good. Facing your weaknesses, for example, is often difficult and heavy, and yet in many cases self-acceptance brings God closer and comes with an increase in trust and charity. Furthermore, following the right path does not automatically mean that God is near (yet it does help).[36] As we know from experience, truly good people are sometimes affected by evil. And who can claim to be following the right path uncompromisingly? Or who follows a purely evil path?

---

35 *Spiritual Exercises*, no. 326.
36 In the 'Rules for Discernment', Ignatius makes a difference between those who follow the right path and those who do not, specifying that, initially, the former receive consolation from God and are harassed by the devil, and vice versa for the latter. While this is a useful distinction, the spiritual life is also very complex and unclear, as Ignatius is well aware. See *Spiritual Exercises*, nos. 314 315, cf. however no. 322.

Let's return once more to Sister Anne. It is very much possible that God speaks through her frustrations. Maybe God is saying through her loneliness and her cold heart that she is no longer in the right place? Could God invite her to seek a life elsewhere, perhaps? That would mean that ultimately the frustration is something positive: it is an aspect of a saving journey. In that case, you will probably find under the layer of frustrations another layer of inspiration. Your task as spiritual companion will be to listen to the frustration in such a way that this hidden layer emerges from the shadows into the full light. After paying some attention to Anne's frustrations, the spiritual companion will explore, together with her, what is happening in that layer of inspiration. What does her new perspective look like? How exactly is God speaking? In this way, that which leads to life is being privileged.

But it is also possible that Anne's loneliness and her cold heart are a sign that an ill wind is blowing. In that case, Anne's experiences indicate that, instead of God speaking to her, she is being influenced by evil. The results of evil at work are apparent: she has gone from considerate gentleness to cold hardness, from light to darkness, from life to death. In such a case, the spiritual director searches in vain for a deeper layer of inspiration. As soon as it becomes clear what she is dealing with, the director should hear the alarm bell ringing. Delving deeper into the frustrations will not make it any better. No good layers will appear, on the contrary. Rubbing a stain makes it worse, not better. There is only one way forward: to fundamentally change direction. (Ways to shift the direction are discussed in Chapters 4, 5, 7 and 8.)

Privileging salvation, life, and God sounds simple yet is complex in practice. To illustrate how radical the confusion can be, let me give another example. In 'A Pilgrim's Journey', a variety of autobiography, Ignatius shares what seemed to be an experience of God that turned out to be the contrary. At a certain point, after his adventurous plan to live and work in the Holy Land came to nothing, Ignatius turned to studies. That started with the dull task of learning the academic language of his time, Latin. As he set out to do so, the following happened:

when he began to commit things to memory, as is necessary at the beginning of language study, new insights into spiritual things would occur to him, and new enjoyments, and this in so powerful a way that he couldn't learn by heart, nor could he get rid of the insights however much he resisted them.[37]

On the face of it, God encouraged Ignatius in the undoubtedly not very glorious experience of going back to school, himself in his thirties, with teenagers for his company. God seemed to accompany him too, bestowing insights and spiritual taste. Hallelujah! Except for the fact that Ignatius couldn't manage to get his homework done. After some reflection, it dawned upon him that the consolations may well be a temptation. This insight was confirmed for Ignatius when, after a kind of confession to his teacher, including a solemn promise to fulfil his duties, the temptation disappeared.[38] What seemed truly divine turned out to be the opposite.

The Angel of Light and the Angel of Darkness
The examples of Anne and Ignatius make it clear that the preference for what leads to life presupposes a theoretical, spiritual-theological framework. It is assumed that in the human soul two forces are at work. One brings salvation, life, light; the other brings the opposite. It doesn't matter much what you call these forces: good and evil, God and the devil, light and darkness. (More esoteric names such as good energy and bad energy also point in the right direction, but I'm not sure that they sufficiently convey the full Christian story.) The examples illustrate that having the intention to pay attention to what is good and of God is not sufficient, as these forces have different manifestations. A good spiritual companion is aware of that and treats every spiritual experience with a healthy dose of distrust. He knows that God may be present in unexpected manifestations and that devil constantly needs to be unmasked. Not everything that seems beneficial is so, and sometimes what seems unholy is beneficial. Or in Ignatius's terms, the angel of

---
37 'Reminiscences or Autobiography', no. 54, in *Personal Writings*, p. 39.
38 'Reminiscences or Autobiography', no. 55, in *Personal Writings*, p. 39.

darkness 'takes on the appearance of an angel of light'.[39]

To be able to choose what is good and salutary, you first have to determine what you are dealing with. If it is of God and for salvation, you embrace it; and if it is not, you leave it. In other words, the spiritual-theological framework of the two spiritual forces also involves so-called discernment of spirits*. Basically, discernment means that you analyse the inspirations and inner movements of each experience. That may sound spiritual and contemplative, yet discernment is ultimately a highly practical matter. The discernment of spirits matters because of its practical usefulness. The goal is not merely insight, but to choose on the basis of that insight between what is good and salutary and what is not. This is evident in Ignatius' description of what the rules of discernment are:

> Rules to aid us toward perceiving and then understanding, at least to some extent, the various motions which are caused in the soul: the good motions that they may be received and the bad that they may be rejected.[40]

First you have to experience or 'feel' the movements, then to understand or 'recognise' them, and finally to act practically: to 'receive' or to 'reject'. (In most cases, letting go is better than actively rejecting; the risk of the latter is to spend too much time and energy on it.)

To summarise, we saw that because of conflicting inner forces the preference for salvation, life and God is in fact complicated and calls for the discernment of the spirits. How does that work concretely? How do you notice what is going on? What should you be paying attention to? What is the legend or key that tells you what you are dealing with? How do you unmask deceit? More on that follows later (see particularly

---

39 *Spiritual Exercises*, no. 332. This is typically one of the rules for discernment from the Second Series, as the difference between good and bad gets more subtle. Full text: 'It is characteristic of the evil angel, who takes on the appearance of an angel of light, to enter by going along the same way as the devout soul and then to exit by his own way with success for himself. That is, he brings good and holy thoughts attractive to such an upright soul and then strives little by little to get his own way, by enticing the soul over to his own hidden deceits and evil intentions'. In the case of Ignatius, that meant, making sure Ignatius would not learn Latin, so he would not be able to pursue his studies.
40 *Spiritual Exercises*, no. 313.

Chapter 7). For now, let me once again conclude with a comment on asceticism, because privileging what leads to life requires a serious dose of self-renunciation. For all our reactions and considerations, we must ask ourselves whether they are inspired by this preference for God and what is good, or not. Of course, this is a principle, not an absolute rule; it does not rule out also paying some attention to difficulties, issues, and sin. More on that follows later, too (particularly in Chapters 4, 5, and 7).

(4) Formation for Spiritual Maturity

Gradually a picture emerges of what spiritual accompaniment is. It begins with respect for how God communicates with the person one accompanies. The next principle involves being interested in spiritual experience with – thirdly – a preference for what is good and what is of God. One last core value completes the quartet: formation for spiritual maturity.

Formation is like looking at an atlas or a map with a child. You explain to the child that this is meadow, that is forest, here a river flows, and there is a city. If you really want to help the child, you also say that you know all of this because light green stands for meadow, dark green for forest, light blue for water and grey or brown for city. If you teach the child to understand the legend, you give him insight such that the child is no longer dependent on you, but from now on he can read the map himself.

The same goes for spiritual direction. It is important that you share the legend. In this way, the person that you accompany understands what you are doing, why you are asking about one thing and not another, why you are surprised or happy, and so on. You teach people the way to their souls and how to find orientation in their souls in such a way that they are aware of the path you are taking together. Spiritual accompaniment is a kind of mystagogy: an initiation into something hidden and secret. But you're not supposed to keep the secret to yourself. You're not a medicine man or a medium. Your authority isn't based on what you know and the other doesn't. You would rather mediate and initiate, so that the person you accompany can grow up. The result will be that he is able to detect himself the signs that indicate where you are on the map, or, she herself will have insight into her inner experiences.

For example, Sister Anne may be hopefully and joyfully looking forward to a new life outside the monastery. After some further listening you should enquire with a healthy dose of suspicion – after all, hope and joy can be deceptive – if that joy and hope have something to do with God and salvation, or not. Maybe Anne finds your approach annoying. Why do you ask all those questions? Why do you want to know what she hopes for and how she imagines this new life? Why do you ask for personal details, such as how she prays and what she experiences in prayer? Why do you push her to say more? In that scenario, it's better to explain a little bit about what you are doing and why. If Anne knows what is going on, that you are guiding her and helping her to know her own soul, she may be able to let go of her annoyance and open up to the process. For example, you could explain that you are interested in her spiritual experiences and their subtleties because these experiences often disclose something about how God is at work. Even in the case that Anne does not have any resistance and simply trusts your questions, it can be good for her spiritual maturity if you explain the process. In this way, you are helping Anne to get to know the legend of her soul.

The theoretical framework of this approach is in fact very simple. You believe in the other person's capacity to grow up and to become spiritually mature, and to understand the journey for herself. Because you believe in this latent capacity, you help the other person to learn and use a spiritual legend. By implication, you do not cultivate relationships in which people depend on you and your expertise. That immediately makes clear what the temptation is and why it is difficult to do this: you make yourself less necessary. If a child knows the legend of the map himself, he doesn't need you anymore. As soon as Anne begins to find her way in her soul herself, she needs you less. Yet that is exactly what we humans want so much: to be useful, to be necessary. So this too requires some serious asceticism. Spiritual accompaniment is not about what I need but about what helps the other person to get acquainted with the hidden, beautiful, yet deceptive world of the soul.

In my pastoral work, I have noticed both that formation (as it is meant here) is an important value for spiritual direction, and that it should not become too central. Spiritual direction is not a lecture or lesson. Therefore, your input and explanations should be measured.

In the writings of the first Jesuits we may see traces of this type of formation. In the introductory notes to the *Spiritual Exercises* for example, Ignatius suggests the spiritual director may give the directee some instruction on spiritual discernment if he feels that such would be helpful. In his own words: 'The Eighth. According to the need perceived in the exercitant with respect to the desolations and deceptive tactics of the enemy, and also the consolations, the giver of the Exercises may explain to the retreatant the rules of the First and Second weeks for recognising the different kinds of spirits (in nos. 313–327 and nos. 328–336)'.[41] Does Ignatius hope that, by sharing the legend, the accompanied person will grow in insight and better understand himself or his soul?

Perhaps Pierre Favre's testimony contains traces of this type of instruction. Favre, one of Ignatius's first companions, had a very fine and sensitive soul and as a result suffered from scruples. In his spiritual autobiography called *Memoriale*, he remembers gratefully, in the form of a spiritual 'note to self', that Ignatius helped him to calm his restless soul by giving him understanding. The way he describes Ignatius's help suggests a form of teaching:

> May it please the divine clemency to give me the grace of clearly remembering and pondering the benefits which the Lord conferred on me in those days through that man. Firstly, he gave me an understanding of my conscience and of the temptations and scruples I had for so long without either understanding them or seeing the way by which I would be able to get peace.[42]

---

41 *Spiritual Exercises*, no. 8.
42 *The Spiritual Writings of Pierre Favre. The Memoriale and Selected Letters and Instructions* (St. Louis: The Institute of Jesuit Sources, 1996), p. 65, no. 9. For more about Favre, see Brian O'Leary, *Pierre Favre and Discernment. The Discernment of Spirits in the* Memoriale *of Blessed Peter Favre*, 2nd rev. ed. (Oxford: Way Publications, 2006). Cf. Jos Moons, 'Remembering as a Crucial Spiritual Tool. Pierre Favre's Spiritual Life according to the Memoriale', in *The Way. A Review of Christian Spirituality Published by the British Jesuits* 55/2 (2016), pp. 71–81.

Favre added that, over time, he became more and more familiar with his various inner movements and that he began to feel and find out the evil spirit.[43] That means that Favre matured in such a way that he himself started to have insight, so that he needed Ignatius less. It seems Favre was able to do so on the basis of some instruction that he received from Ignatius.

A Concrete Method

So how do you respond to Anne, the Trappistine religious sister whom I introduced at the beginning of this chapter and who was going through a grave crisis? In the first place, because of God's secret dealings with each person, you treat her with great reverence. In the second place, you are particularly interested in what is happening in her soul and thirdly, you privilege those inner movements that have to do with God and are salvific. Finally, you periodically explain what you are doing and why in order to form her spiritual maturity.

These are four core values of spiritual accompaniment from an Ignatian perspective. Together they form an image, an ideal, a kind of vision: this is what spiritual accompaniment should look like. Or if you prefer factual language, they make up a definition. Spiritual accompaniment is, as Barry and Connolly write:

> Help given by one believer to another that enables the latter to pay attention to God's personal communication to him or her, to respond to this personally communicating God, to grow in intimacy with this God, and to live out the consequences of the relationship.[44]

This also makes clear what spiritual direction is not. It is not a pastoral conversation full of understanding for the other person's ordeal and giving advice should not be its major element. The experienced spiritual directors Barry and Connolly especially warn beginning directors that

---
43 See *The Spiritual Writings of Pierre Favre*, pp. 64–67, nos. 8–13.
44 Barry, Connolly, *The Practice of Spiritual Direction*, p. 8.

spiritual accompaniment is not about proclaiming doctrine or moral teaching either: 'We have found it necessary to stress this point because of the almost universal and deeply entrenched tendency of ministering people to want to inculcate truth, to teach, to instruct. This tendency rears its head so quickly that beginning spiritual directors often do not listen well to the experience of their directees'.[45] You have a very specific and essentially simple agenda: to talk about God as lived and experienced in the soul, not about God as a theoretical or theological idea.[46]

Although I believe that these principles matter, they do not in and of themselves form a practice of spiritual accompaniment. It is like having a Church that says, 'We want to be a welcoming community'. That, of course, is a wonderful ideal. But what is that Church really going to do to be hospitable? It's also like someone saying, 'I want to live a healthy life'. How is she going to make that happen? So how does spiritual accompaniment work concretely?

In the chapters that follow, I will develop these four values into a concrete and practical program for practicing Ignatian spiritual accompaniment. The program consists of six tools: 1. Taking it Easy; 2. Listening by Following; 3. Searching for the Soul; 4. Going Deeper; 5. Evaluating; 6. Forming for Spiritual Maturity. The objective is this: without any rush to dwell extensively on the other person's life and soul, especially on inner experiences, with particular attention to spiritual discernment, and with some attention also to formation.[47] In each chapter I will elaborate one of those tools, illustrating with various case studies how they could be used, so that this becomes indeed 'A Guide to Ignatian Practice'.

---

45 Barry, Connolly, *The Practice of Spiritual Direction*, pp. 43–44.
46 Barry and Connolly helpfully illustrate the difference by outlining how one may respond to somebody in mourning in the context of spiritual accompaniment and pastoral accompaniment, see *The Practice of Spiritual Direction*, pp. 78–82. Cf. the two examples at pp. 155–159 that illustrate too that you should start with exploring and deepening rather than giving advice.
47 Cf. the proposal elaborated by Bernardo Olivera, with the following concrete tools (that he calls functions): 1. Welcome (that is, welcoming and accepting the other for whom he is); 2. Clarification; 3. Confrontation; 4. Discernment. His proposal is very much worth reading yet illustrates that the focus on spiritual experience – which Olivera's model does not have – is a distinctive feature of Ignatian spiritual accompaniment. See Olivera, *Light for my path*, pp. 20–21 and pp. 33–108. Cf. my earlier comment on confrontation.

3: FIRST TOOL

TAKING IT EASY

The first tool for spiritual direction that I would like to present is to take it easy.[48] The intimate work of the soul takes time; it requires some warming up. Anyone who tries to get down to business too quickly will shoot himself in the foot. The spiritual director should bear this in mind and should try to take it easy.

Imagine the following situation. Mark, forty years of age, e-mailed to ask for a talk with Hanna, his spiritual director. He explained that he wanted to talk about prayer. He felt a desire for prayer, but every time he tried to pray, it did not work. He didn't know what to do, and silence was difficult. Mark and Hanna made an appointment. However, when they meet, Mark starts to talk about all kinds of other things instead of addressing his difficulties with prayer and silence. He chats about his children and how they get good grades at school. He is so grateful for that. Work is another topic: he loves the projects he is involved in, although he is somewhat disappointed in his colleagues. Hanna decides to let it go for a while. Gently 'humming' – *hmm, yes, hmm* – she goes with the flow of Mark's story. Yet after fifteen minutes she kindly intervenes: 'Mark, so far, we've talked about your children, about their school, about your work, and about some other things …'. Before she is able to complete her sentence, Mark says, 'Yes, that's right, I wanted to talk about prayer'.

---

48 I skip a few practical matters, such as: where do you receive the directee, how often do you meet, what about remuneration, the issue of confidentiality, etc. These are important matters, yet this book focuses 'only' on tools.

This case illustrates that the directee often needs to 'warm up'. Spiritual accompaniment involves a change of gears. We move from daily humdrum and business, where we stay at the surface level, toward the soul and its delicate intimacy. That move takes time. It's better not to rush it. The spiritual companion shouldn't hastily bring an end to the chatter and get down to business. With subjects as private as spiritual life, the soul, faith, and God, a person needs to take their time. Small talk is a time of preparation to hear each other's voice, see each other's face and eyes, get used to the space and become comfortable. Thus, small talk prepares for a second, more substantive phase of the conversation. By the way, the directee may not be the only one who needs this, because the director also needs to acclimatise.

In this chapter I would like to elaborate this tool of taking it easy. Firstly, I will focus on how it works concretely. How do you take it easy? Then I will discuss how you make the transition to the subject matter. How do you actually get started with the spiritual direction itself? After that I introduce another case to illustrate that in all of this God, without being explicitly mentioned, most certainly has a place. Finally, I broaden the theme by briefly discussing the importance of maintaining a kind of relaxation during the whole conversation, not just at the start.

Small Talk

The first tool basically boils down to friendly small talk. With students you can talk about their lectures and exams. If someone has just moved houses you ask about the move, and if someone has just changed jobs you talk about the new job. With monks you talk about their life in the monastery (about the vegetable garden or the renovation, and whether it is busy with guests), with young mothers and fathers about their children and how it is to be a parent. When it rains you ask if it was very wet on the way here, when the sun shines you say something about the nice weather, and at Easter time you may start with that. You don't have an agenda except for warming up.

Sometimes you don't have to take the initiative for small talk, as the directee gets the chitchat going. Other people might be a bit uncomfortable at the start of their session of spiritual accompaniment. That's when you need to step in with some small talk that prepares the ground for a deeper conversation later on. It is best to put on an imperturbable smile, at least in a figurative sense, and resolve not to be discouraged by the other person's tangible discomfort. Your resolved warmth and friendliness can help the other person thaw out.

As a side note, when I receive spiritual accompaniment myself, I still like it when we start with small talk. The spiritual world is not new to me, I am not afraid of self-reflection and introspection, nor do I feel uncomfortable with my spiritual companion. It's just nice to be able to land before we start.

Plunging into the Depths

There comes a moment that you should make the transition from small talk to spiritual direction proper. After some warming up, it is time for the plunge. If that transition does not come about by itself, it's the director's job to take the initiative.

Take that initiative only after giving space and time for the growing familiarity of small talk and do it as gently as possible. The lighter you steer to the depth, the better. The phrase 'so far we've talked about …' from Mark's case is a very light intervention. Doing no more than summarising, Hanna suggested that she was rounding off one part of the conversation and gave the hint at the possibility of changing the topic. In the case of Mark, it turned out to be sufficient. Mark understood the hint before Hanna finished her sentence and immediately turned the conversation to the topic of prayer. That's instructive: during small talk the directee rarely forgets what he has really come for.

Sometimes you need to insist somewhat and to be more forceful in steering to the depths. It's best to do that as calmly and tenderly as possible. Imagine that Mark was resistant to geting started with the actual spiritual direction. In that case, you could have used the information that was at your disposal. You knew the reason for the conversation, so you could have said, for example, 'I believe you said that another thing that's going on for you is related to prayer'. Probably, that would be enough. You specify clearly yet humbly what Mark himself had stated. It is rare that you need to do more. Something like 'What are you here for?' risks sounding cold and coercive and thereby ineffective. People don't lower their guard on command.

God in Everyday Experience

Maybe you are thinking, 'This is a waste of my time! Why should I take it easy?' After all, the director and the directee both know why they're meeting. Why not get down to business and simply start? In my experience, this period of warming up is in no way a waste of time. Small talk is more than a useless prelude. Just as the prelude contains a rehearsal of all the important musical themes that follow, so does the time of warming up. Small talk matters. In fact, upon closer consideration, it is already about God.

Take the loving, patient attitude of the spiritual director. That attitude speaks volumes, even without naming God. Perhaps you have heard the saying attributed to Francis of Assisi, 'Preach the Gospel at all times; when necessary, use words'? That is what you are doing here. God is part of ordinary small talk, present in the space that you offer and in the patience you radiate.

Moreover, what is discussed during small talk can point out what is going on in the soul; thereby it may lead to God. In that way too, ordinary chitchat may have to do with God.

Imagine Esther, a mother of three small children and the head of personnel in a regional hospital. She meets up with Renata, a lay pastoral worker and an experienced spiritual director. When they sit together, Esther passionately relates all of her recent ventures: the renovation of the barn that was overseen by her husband, the changes at her workplace, the fact that her second child has already started going to school. She is delighted that her family has such a good time on the weekends: she usually bakes a cake with the children, he makes coffee, then they all work together in the garden, and so on. In previous conversations, prayer had been an important theme. Renata therefore wonders if she should ask how prayer is going now, but she decides not to intervene too

First Tool: Taking It Easy

quickly and wait and see for a while. Is Esther telling all this by way of an introduction or is there more to it? Is she – and is Renata – perhaps on spiritual ground already? As Renata is not sure, she takes it easy for a moment. The dialogue then develops as follows:

R: So many things happening, Esther! (*with a smile*) You're busy!
E: Yeah, indeed. I feel a lot of energy. At the end of the day I am tired, so I go to bed on time; the next day I get up refreshed. (*quiet for a moment*) I am so ... well, I guess, so happy to have so much energy.
R: You have a lot of energy and you are happy with that.
E: Yes. In fact, if I can be honest with you, I consider it a special grace. I feel strong, I can do a lot: my work, taking care of the children, everything.
R: Yes, I'm impressed that you do so much! And you said (*pauses for a moment*) that you consider it a grace?
E: Um, yeah. (*quiet for a moment*) I mean I see it as a gift. I strongly feel that I don't just do it myself. I'm given strength; I receive it.

This short conversation illustrates how a seemingly ordinary story may turn out to be more than that. Esther's active and energetic life appears to have an unexpected depth. She feels that her energy is a gift. Small talk is not really small after all. It can be very spiritual.

Taking It Easy with God

So far I've explained that it's good to take it easy and to be patient in your search for depth. Now I want to add that this also applies to God. With God too you should take it easy, as you should do with other explicitly faith-related themes. It is better not to speed ahead and introduce the subject of God or prayer, faith and grace. These are intimate matters, and they need some warming up to. The risk that these subjects will be forgotten is minimal. After all, this is not a chance meeting; the directee came to you or spoke to you as a spiritual director. It is almost self-evident that you will eventually talk about God. The cases above of Mark and Hanna and Esther and Renata show that you don't have to worry about 'forcing' a spiritual conversation to be about God.

In addition, by taking your time, you increase the chance that you will talk about God *better*. The next few sentences from Esther and Renata's conversation demonstrate how that works.

> E: Um, yeah. (*quiet for a moment*) I mean I see it as a gift. I strongly feel that I don't just do it myself. I'm given strength; I receive it.
>
> R: You receive it. (*pauses*) What kind of experience is that 'receiving' you just spoke of?
>
> E: What a beautiful question! It's a bit like a friend coming by unexpectedly, and then we have coffee and cake in the garden, and everything is well.
>
> R: So you're unexpectedly catching up, in the garden, and then things are well.
>
> E: Yes, that's how it is.
>
> R: And when things are well, what happens? What do you feel?
>
> E: It's very still and very overwhelming at the same time. This unexpected encounter was really nice. It brought some sort of a calm peace. Yet it was overwhelming too, because in all its simplicity it was so rich. It's like finding flowers everywhere: in the kitchen, in the living room, at work, in the bedroom, on the stairs. Almost too good to be true.
>
> R: So when you say that your energy is a gift, a grace, that it's like someone who comes to visit, and things are well.
>
> E: Yes, after such a meeting I feel very energetic again, very rich. (*smiles*) Then I can take on the world again!
>
> R: (*with a smile*) And from what I'm hearing, that's exactly

what you do, take on the world! (*pauses*) Does God have something to do with that energy, with that experience?
E: Well, I think so. But I'm not totally sure. It's not as if I see a Jesus-figure in a white robe, speaking to me.
R: So there's no Jesus-figure?
E: No.
R: And no God either, really?
E: Well, maybe God. I feel that the energy I receive is caring and loving. I can do a lot of good with it. I think I see something of God in that.

This part of Esther and Renata's conversation demonstrates how the topic of God may come up almost by itself. Esther's spiritual director took it easy and waited until she felt that the time had come to see if she was right in suspecting that there was a deeper layer. Words like 'grace' and 'gift' suggested that Esther was saying much more than simply relating her day-to-day activities. This example shows the spiritual gains that may come with taking it easy. In this conversation, who God is and how he interacts with us are determined by what is happening in Esther's life and soul. God reveals himself to Esther through a very personal experience of grace, energy and love instead of through (preconceived) ideas taken from Scripture or theology. God is revealed here-and-now, not so much as a white-robed figure, but rather as a caring and loving presence.

In stronger terms, that means that if you bring up the topic of God too quickly, the conversation risks being too little about God. If the directee were to talk about God in an early stage of the conversation, she will quite probably say something perfunctory on the basis of common faith-convictions rather than personal faith-experiences. In other words, if you rush ahead with the subject of God, you may make it more difficult for God to reveal his face here and now. If you wait and first talk about experience before you address the topic of God, he reveals himself in his actual relationship with the directee.

Relaxation

Until now I have talked about taking it easy, warming up, patience, and not speeding into the topic of God. Another useful word is relaxation. Instead of getting down to business quickly, the spiritual companion should be relaxed. That is not just something for the early stages of the conversation but should be a feature of the whole session. For example, after something vulnerable has been said, a smile, a small joke or an anecdote can provide some breathing space or break the suspension. The dialogue between Esther and Renata gives some examples of this kind of relaxation. For example, Renata reacted with a smile to Esther saying she could take on the world. In this way she created a simple, short *intermezzo* before picking up the thread by asking if God had something to do with that. Small jokes can also be part of relaxation. You have to find your own way and to see what suits yourself, the directee and the situation. Obviously, delicacy is of the utmost importance. If you add a light touch to the conversation, it has to be right: laughing *at* somebody is out of the question, as is laughing away something serious.

Finally, it is important to say that you sometimes have to practice patience and relaxation for a longer period of time. Some people need a few conversations to warm up, to trust you, or to get in touch with themselves. In those cases, your motto should be *calm down and stay relaxed*, without getting frustrated or doubting yourself. Do not be afraid that God is not working in the life and soul of the other. Do not be afraid that God will not come up in the discussion. The greater your patience and relaxation, the greater the chance that you will witness the reality of God's presence in the directee's experiences.

4: SECOND TOOL

LISTENING BY FOLLOWING

After the warming up, the real work starts. It begins with what I like to call *listening by following*; this is our second tool. Although not the core of spiritual accompaniment – more about that later – listening and following are essential; they are the foundation.

How does this second tool work concretely? To demonstrate this, let me introduce you to Maria, a nineteen-year-old student of psychology in Birmingham; she is living with her parents in Coventry and was brought up as a Roman Catholic. Lately she finds it hard to believe and wonders if God really exists. A conversation with her mother didn't help much, and now she wants to hear what Father Pete, the pastor of her home parish, has to say about this. Pete, a cheerful man in his late forties, welcomes Maria and walks her to the parlor. After they have talked for a bit about homework and other student stuff, Pete gently attempts to end the warming up:

P: Well, I'm glad to hear that you're happy with your studies and that you are meeting nice people. It sounds like it is the right place for you.
M: Yeah, indeed. But there's something else that I wanted to talk about with you.
P: Okay, I'm listening.

Notice how easy it is to make the transition from small talk to the 'real' spiritual direction. Pete's summarising intervention, which steered slightly towards a conclusion, is enough to invite Maria to get down to business: 'there's something else that I wanted to talk about'.

> M: Ummm, how should I put it? (*pauses; then speaks softly*) Sometimes I'm not sure that God exists. (*pauses; then looks at Pete*) And I had thought, well, I'm sure that you can help me with that.
> P: Ah, so sometimes you doubt and wonder: does God really exist?
> M: Yes, I'm not so sure. It could all be an invention, couldn't it?
> P: Hmm.
> M: And then I talked to my mother about it, and she told me to that I should simply believe. Believing isn't the same as knowing, she explained.
> P: (*smiles*)
> M: (*sighs*) That didn't help me much ...
> P: That didn't help?
> M: No, not at all.
> P: So, if I understand you correctly, you're in doubt as to whether God exists, and when you shared that with your mother who was offering a solution, that wasn't really a solution; it did not work for you.

In this conversation Pete's strategy is to consistently follow Maria. Wherever she goes, he goes too. When she doubts about God's existence, Pete joins her in that: 'Ah, so sometimes you doubt and wonder: does God exist?' Discreetly and deliberately, he is not trying to 'save' Maria from her doubt, he simply acknowledges the question. When she persists in her doubt and suggests that God could have been made up, again he simply hums by way of acknowledgement, without providing a solution. When she starts talking about her mother, he follows again, first by smiling and then by repeating that the conversation with her mother did not help. This form of listening by following is the foundation of the art of spiritual accompaniment.

In the remainder of this chapter I want to explain this technique further. Then I will discuss the experience that people often don't say what is really happening but rather hide. What is the best way to react in those case? Three evaluative reflections bring this chapter to a close.

Active Listening: What to Avoid

Listening by following as Pete did with Maria is not *just* listening. It's not simply allowing the other person to talk while I do not. No, rather, it's me listening while the other person talks. To make it clear that this is an activity, often an adjective is added: active listening. This implies that there is also passive listening, as there is bad listening.

Active listening principally means to listen by following your conversation partner. You should go with the flow, overcoming any personal resistance that you may feel about the direction that the conversation is going in or coming from. The key here is to let go of fear, frustration, judgement, etc. In this case, don't be afraid of Maria's doubt and of her apparent disbelief. As this is not as obvious as it sounds, I will give a few examples of bad listening: things you usually shouldn't do.

The first thing you should avoid is filling in the blanks. Don't assume that you understand what is being said or left unsaid. Once, when I had broken my left hand, a colleague said to me, 'Luckily it wasn't your right hand'. Filling in this way is undesirable in general, and certainly in the context of spiritual accompaniment. While the focus of the conversation should be what the directee says (and is trying to say), by filling in the conversation with my own experiences, convictions or ideas, I refocus the conversation on me. So don't say to Maria, 'Yes, I can understand that very well. Your life is changing a lot, including God'. Really, you don't know if that's the issue for Maria. Of course, you may in your mind sense – in silence – that this could be a possible interpretation of Maria's faith crisis. At the appropriate moment, you may even suggest it to her. But you must not assume that until you have heard Maria. For example, you could enquire how she experiences the changes in her life, and if she doesn't really know, you may suggest possibilities: are the changes uncomfortable, difficult, exciting, sad, lonely? However, you must remain very open to other interpretations. What matters is not what you think, but what the directee thinks.

Secondly, avoid saving and solving. Neither saving nor solving are forms of active listening, on the contrary. It's like when you are at a wine store. While explaining the kind of red wine you're looking for, the shopkeeper keeps interrupting you, insisting that you must have this bottle. You begin to sense that the shopkeeper is really saying, 'I don't have time to listen to you; let me quickly solve this for you, so that I can go on with my "to do list"'. If you try to solve Maria's problem, you are basically saying, 'Please, I can't stand your struggle, spare me your suffering. Pray a little more, then it'll pass. Shall I walk you to the door now?' That's what her mother did. Clearly it wasn't what Maria needed.

Thirdly, avoid cutting off. Especially in the first phase of the conversation, you better let the directee talk about what he wants in the way he wants. You give him space. If the directee wants to specify all sorts of unnecessary and tiring details of an illness, you listen. If someone sighs about the bishop or her husband or children, you give space for that. Only after a while, if it continues, you can aim for more depth. For example, you may summarise and then say, 'I see that it is important for you that I hear this from you'. Or you say that in the form of a question: 'Why do you find it important to share this with me?' In that way you're not saying that something is unimportant, but you are exploring why it is significant. (By way of comment, while steering towards the deep end, you should avoid an implicit evaluation, for example, by suggesting that the focus on these medical details is excessive or that the complaints are unreasonable.)

Last but not least: no pious cheering up, please. That form of spiritualising forces a 'holier' perspective upon the directee. In the case of Maria's doubt, for example, spiritualising would be linking her experience to the mystical tradition of not knowing. Other possible forms of pious cheering up would be to speak about disbelief and doubt in Scripture: the disbelief of the Jewish people in the desert or Jesus' doubts in the garden of Gethsemane. Later in the conversation, pointing out these possibilities could be really useful – as possibilities, introduced in the form of a question – but at this moment it is much too early for that. Ironically, a spiritual perspective that comes too early or is forced upon the directee is spiritually disrespectful and simply violent. Instead of respecting what is going on in the directee's soul and honoring how God is at work here, you push aside the directee's story and force your ideas upon her or him. The fact that it is done with good intentions does not make it less sad, for spirituality should not be used to overpower and silence.

All these bad examples suffer from the same flaw: you are not following the other person but yourself. Your reaction is determined by *your* thoughts, by *your* practical approach, by *your* impatience or agenda. Listening therefore requires asceticism. You must renounce yourself to make space for the other person.

Active Listening: What to Do

So how can we listen well? The core of active listening is this: showing that you have really heard and understood the other person and that you accept what has been said. This can be done in different ways. The lightest form of active listening is non-verbal and consists of (mainly) bodily responses such as nodding or smiling. These are reassuring and inviting signals that tell the directee that what he has said has been heard and is okay. As a result, he senses that he can say more, that he can move on. Other light forms of active listening are the hardly verbal response of humming, 'hmm', or utterances like 'ah yes' or 'really'. No matter how light these kinds of responses are, they will not fail to have an effect. Because they signal to the directee that he has been heard, he will therefore continue to speak. The case of Maria and Pete is a case in point.

A second form of active listening is what conversation technique jargon calls 'mirroring' or 'reflecting'. It is somewhat clearer that this is an active form of listening as it involves an activity on the part of the spiritual director. He or she repeats what the directee said, in more or less the same terms. For example, after Maria has expressed her questions regarding the existence of God, Pete reacts with almost identical words: 'Ah, so sometimes you doubt and wonder: does God really exist?' He did the same when Maria told her mother's advice was useless, echoing 'That didn't help'.

Often you can be brief, especially in the later stages of the conversation, when the conversation has gained some depth. Then one word may well be sufficient. For example, if someone says that lately he has been feeling a real connection with God (or with his partner), you could simply respond, 'A real connection'. That is enough to confirm that you are with him, and thus invite him to say more.

I should add that mirroring is not only about what is said but also about body language and emotions, for example when someone bursts into tears. After you have reassured them that it is okay to cry, provided a glass of water or tissues, and when the person has calmed down a bit, you can say, for example, 'That touched you, didn't it?' This also applies if someone looks very happy and you make an observation about their joy. What exactly you say, of course, depends on the specific emotional landscape. By means of your mirroring, you are letting the directee know: 'You are okay; please, feel free to say something more, if you wish'.

You may also mirror larger chunks of the conversation; that is a third form of mirroring, which in fact takes the form of paraphrasing. In the case study, Pete did this in the final sentence: 'So, if I understand you correctly, you're in doubt as to whether God exists, and when you shared that with your mother, who was offering a solution, that wasn't really a solution; it did not work for you'. This form of active listening tells the directee – in this case, Maria – that she has been heard, that her story has been accepted, and thereby invites her to say more.

Where I recommended earlier to keep your responses as short as possible, here I need to add that mirroring bigger chunks sometimes takes longer, as indeed we saw in the example of Maria. Mirroring on a larger scale is particularly useful for linking various elements or parts of the conversation. For example, the spiritual director may indicate a tension between one experience or statement and another. Or she may suggest that (or wonder if) one event explains another. In this way the spiritual companion searches for structure. This helps the person who is receiving accompaniment to grasp her story and to choose what she wants to say, what is most important, what stands out, etc.

Finally, a fourth form of active listening works by asking questions. For example, you may ask, 'You've shared a few things now; what was most important?' Or you may enquire how these things are linked (if at all), what stays most with the directee, how she looks back on it now, and so on. You stick to what has been shared yet invite the directee to revisit it and to say a bit more. In that sense, it resembles the other forms of active listening. Yet asking questions quite a heavy form of reacting and one in which the director herself is more involved by suggesting an approach or direction. Therefore, you have to be very moderate in using this form of active listening. If lighter interventions are possible, show preference for those.

Hiding

Sometimes, the directee will want to nuance what you mirror, or even to correct or to deny it. Please allow the directee all the space he wants to do that. After all, you are following, aren't you? If the person you are accompanying wants to go somewhere else, just go with him. That's why a light question mark at the end of your interventions is not a bad idea. For example: 'Ah, so sometimes you doubt and wonder: does God really exist?' That leaves the door wide open. You can even make it explicit: 'Ah, let me try. You doubt, you wonder if God exists; is that what you were saying?' Obviously, more important than the question mark is the actual openness.

There are various reasons that the directee may want to nuance, correct or deny. Sometimes he does so because you didn't render the directee's words correctly. But even if you were accurate in what you said, the directee may disagree. Your summary may work as a mirror and provoke a wish for refinement: 'Actually, no, it's more this'. It is important to give space to change, because people often don't say exactly what they mean. That is in part because we like to hide a little, just like children playing hide and seek. People want you to search for them for a while; if you don't, they are disappointed. But they are also disappointed if you don't find them. In other words: if you're searching, they want to be found. If the directee feels that it's safe and that you're interested, he slowly opens up.[49]

It's a bit like Jack, a young theology student at KU Leuven at the end of his first year who was considering quitting. He'd had a hard time. His fellow students were not as friendly as he had hoped. The lecturers did not always respond well to his questions, which – as he readily admitted – weren't always very smart. To make matters worse, his grades were disappointing. When I summarised after some listening that indeed the picture didn't look good, adding that I could imagine that he wanted to quit, Jack reacted fiercely, 'But that's not what I want!' This was a breakthrough and initiated a new type of conversation. We no longer talked about the world outside – fellow students, teachers, results – but about the world of Jack's soul. Eventually, he traded the conversation about things that were making his life difficult for a conversation about beautiful things. At the end of the spiritual direction, a life-giving God had taken center stage, along with light in the soul. Jack discovered that God was whispering to him about keeping courage and about growth, and that in fact He had been doing so for quite some time.

In this case, Jack responded to my summary by denying it: 'But that's not what I want!' It's quite important to note that I had not misunderstood Jack's story or used the wrong words. Rather, my summary functioned as a mirror that showed Jack, to his horror, where he had ended up. It was like a cold shower that woke him up. It recalled – or should I say revealed – another narrative: that he didn't want to stop, that his initial inspiration had faded somewhat but was actually still there, that he found it difficult to adapt, and so on. To use the image of hiding: Jack had hidden himself in a 'I can't so I don't want to' narrative, yet through my persistent searching for him, he allowed himself to be found.

This case shows how important it is that the spiritual director doesn't

---

[49] I owe the image of hiding to Frans van Steenbergen (who uses it more than that he explains what it means for spiritual accompaniment), see 'De geestelijke begeleiding', *Collationes. Vlaams tijdschrift voor theologie en pastoraal* 27 (1997), pp. 393–408, esp. pp. 393–397.

want to be right. It is better to avoid entering into discussion than to insist on being right. Imagine what would have happened if I had repeated that Jack was wrong and that what he had really said was that he didn't want to study anymore. We would have been stuck in the story by which Jack held himself hostage, thereby reducing the chances of Jack's revelation and liberation. Rather, the spiritual companion must be as detached as possible; he follows wherever the other person goes. What you can do is signal that what you hear now sounds very different from what you just heard by adding 'Doesn't it?' By signaling change, you are still following. The phrase 'Doesn't it?' is not about you being right, but about thematising the change you notice in the other person and inviting the other person to engage with that change. It's not about you, it's about the directee.

In addition, Jack's case shows that active listening can be highly transformative. You do not need to push or pull the other person. No need of forbidding, warning, or correcting, 'You shouldn't say that'. No need of holding out a promising alternative: 'Another course of study (or different attitude, or new friends, ...) would be much nicer anyway'. Doing very little is sufficient for bringing about change. Jack realised his turnabout simply (simply?) because he saw the narrative that he himself had just shared and was horrified by it.

In fact, this specific form of listening by following is related to provocative coaching and provocative therapy. In that approach, a coach or therapist plays the role of the devil's advocate. Instead of lending a helping hand or comforting, she goes along with the negative vibes, even developing these further. A coach could say something like, 'I think we should stop our sessions, they lead nowhere'. In Jack's case above, the spiritual director suggested in a provocative manner that it would be better to stop studying theology. Thus, the coach or spiritual companion is not a lifebuoy that prevents the other person from being dragged down by the waves. Rather, the intended effect is that the other person becomes his own lifebuoy. Instead of settling for dependence, you awaken or evoke self-reliance. You stimulate zest for life instead of paralysis. The objective is that he will think indignantly: 'But I want to live!' or 'But I want to study!' or 'But I want to grow!' Needless to say: this presupposes skill, wisdom and a good rapport with the directee.

Finally, Jack's story was a successful one. He let himself be found. Here provocative listening worked, but that's not always the case. You cannot predict how Jack will respond; it is only in hindsight that you realise that the suggestion to stop studying brought about change and was therefore provocative. Moreover, sometimes people prefer the safety of their hideout. Sometimes you will sense that. You will be convinced that there's something more. While it is certainly true that you have other tools at your disposal than the ones discussed so far, it is equally true that you sometimes simply have to wait. Perhaps the other person is not yet ready to be found. Perhaps you're not yet worthy of trust. Never mind. Don't try to break through the other person's shield. It's wise to keep on doing the right thing – listening, following, taking it easy – and to trust that your good work will in time yield its fruits.

Active Listening: A Method or an Art?

The discussion of active listening so far may give the impression that spiritual accompaniment is no more than a technique. But as I said earlier, listening by following establishes the foundation of spiritual accompaniment; it is not its essence. As spiritual accompaniment is something much more subtle, let me make three comments that nuance and evaluate this chapter.

First, how can you ensure that you do more than just applying a technique? How do you practice the *art* of listening? I once accompanied a student who had just followed a few lectures on conversation technique. At one point, she couldn't stand it anymore: she angrily yelled at me that she knew what I was doing. Her reproach resounded with bitterness. She felt that I didn't take her seriously but instead only followed a protocol; I did no more than apply a technique.

Her comments indicate the weakness of what I described above. My emphasis on listening by following and the concrete elaboration of this with techniques indeed raises the question of whether spiritual accompaniment is limited to the application of techniques. The answer is *no*. Techniques are indispensable, but they are no more than a first step. If you are making pancakes for the first time, it's best to scrupulously follow the recipe book. If you are learning to play music, you initially play the music score with mathematical precision. After a while, protocol is complemented by experience. You know the recipe book; you know the music theory. At that moment, technique develops into skill; instead of following rules, you cook, you play. The same goes for listening. The humming, mirroring and paraphrasing of the spiritual director is part of something bigger. It starts with techniques, but it should end as an art. As soon as you thoroughly master the technique, you must forget about it and just (just?) listen.

What about God?[50]

In the second place, how is God part of this? Is listening and following really enough, from a faith perspective? Isn't it important rather in a spiritual conversation to mention God or to suggest a religious theme? Later I will say more about God; here I would like to emphasise that 'just following' conveys a rich faith reality.

Let me start by demythologising the wish to talk about God. At times, this reflex is mainly triggered by our discomfort. We don't find it easy to just stay with the experience of a fellow human being with his or her happiness or troubles. It weighs on us. Therefore, we like to say that it will be all right. Or we give good advice, including good religious advice. (As a matter of fact, it may be really good advice.) All that, however, means that we have found a way around simply hearing and welcoming the other person's story.

If we can bear with our own discomfort, we will find that a lot of good things emerge precisely by *not* bringing up God or offering good advice. By leaving aside our spiritual observations, wise additions, or important corrections, at last we learn to listen. We accept and welcome. Spending time without attempting to bring change or depth brings about a deep revelation (that Karl Rahner would term 'anonymous'); it signals to the

---

[50] In what follows, I make use of a Dutch blog in which I argued that a student chaplain should do 'as little as possible', https://www.igniswebmagazine.nl/spiritualiteit/wat-de-studentenpastor-doet-zo-weinig-mogelijk/ (26-10-2017).

directee that her story and life are worthwhile. That is the Holy Gospel of welcome. A Gospel proclaimed not by many words but by few words: by listening and welcoming.

Sometimes I think this is the deepest layer of what God does: receiving and welcoming. Only after receiving and welcoming does God speak. The same holds true for pastoral and spiritual ministry. For example, a student chaplain most certainly helps students to understand their experiences, often with the help of discernment of the spirits, and a hospital chaplain helps patients with their experiences of despair, loss and powerlessness. But in both cases, the deepest layer of their pastoral service could well be that they accept and welcome.[51]

Following: Always?

So far, I have emphasised that the basis of spiritual accompaniment consists of listening by following and that the tool of active listening is helpful in realising this. To nuance my claim, I added that this tool is meant to develop from a technique into an art and that in all of this God is present, even when God is not named. The third relativising remark addresses the limitations of this approach. While listening by following can be a helpful guide in most cases and while beginning spiritual directors benefit from consciously focusing on this, the director does not always have to follow. He can also help by taking the initiative and introducing certain topics or asking certain questions.

For example, if Maria were to talk about her faith doubts without ever mentioning prayer, it could be useful to kindly invite her to explore that. Does she ever pray? How does she pray? What were her experiences with prayer in the past? And now? The same goes for a seminarian who always talks about his studies but never about prayer. In such a case, you should feel very free to introduce the theme yourself. Evidently it also

---

51 André Louf notes that speaking plainly about what goes on in the soul is an old monastic tradition. That tradition was not primarily about advice or correction or forgiveness, but about openness and acceptance. 'The first relief to offer him [the person that is being accompanied] is permission to exist just as he is, the chance to exist before us just as he experiences himself, even if it is obvious to us that he experiences himself in an incorrect (…) way'. He then refers to *The Little Prince*: 'A friend is above all one who does not judge'. According to Louf, that attitude makes the spiritual director represent God, 'who makes his sun rise on the just and on the sinners'. See *Grace Can Do More*, pp. 75–95, quotes at pp. 78–79.

works the other way around: a seminarian who talks about prayer but not about studies, housemates, or free time. Again, you should feel very free to address these topics. Obviously, you need not do so immediately; there is no hurry. Another example is a father or mother who always talks about the children and never about himself or herself. Or someone who always talks about successes and never about failure. Noticing the gap, an attentive spiritual companion will at the appropriate time and in the appropriate manner take the initiative to discuss it. Although this clearly presupposes more initiative on the part of the spiritual director, you could argue that this is still a form of mirroring. You reflect the other person's story, especially what was not said; you mirror the gap.

Finally, good listeners do by nature all that has been described in this chapter. I still hear my mother saying to my father, sighing upon his return from the office that it was a busy day: 'So you had a busy day today', after which he would continue his story. For most people, however, good active listening does not happen by itself. It takes concerted effort and resolve to respectfully listen and follow another person's story.

Active listening is an important tool but not the only one. As I said at the beginning of this chapter: listening and following are the foundation of spiritual accompaniment, but not the core. That is why I will discuss other, additional tools in the following chapters.

5: THIRD TOOL

SEARCHING FOR SOUL

What does the spiritual director do differently from other caring professionals? All people offering a listening ear to others should, ideally, be calm listeners. In such a way, doctors can inform patients of a correct diagnosis or prescribe an effective course of treatment. Psychologists listen to what is going on underneath the surface of what is said so that they can help to chart a life-giving course with and for their patients. This is also true for therapists, coaches, and pastors. What, then, makes spiritual direction unique? What does a spiritual director do in addition to listening? What is the core of spiritual accompaniment?

From an Ignatian perspective, spiritual accompaniment essentially consists of talking about God on the basis of spiritual experience. In negative terms, spiritual accompaniment is neither a theological conversation, nor even pastoral one. The focus on religious or spiritual experience has to do with the significance of the '*sentir*' that we spoke of earlier (see Chapter 2). As Barry and Connolly noted, spiritual direction is impossible without spiritual experience, in much the same way as one cannot cook without ingredients. A spiritual director's job is therefore to help thematise that experience. He or she is tasked with searching for the soul of the person sitting in front of him or her. In this chapter I will first highlight how this is a specific understanding of spiritual accompaniment. After doing this, I will explain how to search for someone's soul or thematise spiritual experience.

Different Kinds of Spiritual Directors

In an article about the formation of spiritual directors from an Ignatian perspective, the English spiritual director and educator Ruth Holgate identifies three kinds of directors.[52] The first on her list is the experienced mentor: 'the wise, gentle, and strong elder who has seen it all before and can tell us just what we need to hear to navigate this particular stage of our lives – a Dumbledore to our Harry Potter'.[53] A wise old grandparent might exemplify this type of director. If Maria (whom we met in the previous chapter) came for a visit, such a spiritual director, after listening for a bit, would begin to speak of the various changes that a person undergoes in life. He would say that Maria is standing at a crossroads. Naturally, everything is shifting. It would be best if she could let go and simply allow these shifts to happen. The spiritual director would reassure her, 'After some time, everything will be ok'. Maybe, he would illustrate this with examples from his own life or from a book he once read.

Holgate describes the second kind of spiritual director as someone insightful, 'whose intuition is so finely tuned that he or she can see into souls and know just what we need to hear right now'.[54] She can give good advice because of that unique perception. She possesses such insight not by virtue of her life experience, but rather by virtue of her finely attuned sensibility. After listening for a while, she would pose a question to Maria, provide an explanation to something Maria had said, or make a proposal to her. 'Are you working out enough? Are you sensitive to the changing of the seasons? Perhaps the fact that it's now autumn could be playing a role here'. Or maybe, 'Could God be saying something to you?' Maria will notice that what the director says is often right on the mark.

The third kind of spiritual director identified by Holgate is 'the holy prophet who has a direct line to God and can tell us with confidence what God is asking of us and how we should respond'.[55] Such a director is someone who knows God well and who can tell us, in God's name, what would be the best thing for us to do. It seems that Maria hoped

---

52 See Holgate, 'Training Spiritual Directors'.
53 Holgate, 'Training Spiritual Directors', p. 68.
54 Ibid.
55 Ibid.

for such a spiritual director when she went to visit Fr Pete and asked if he could help her because the explanations her mother gave her were not satisfying. Hopefully Pete could say meaningful things concerning prayer, waiting for God, and so forth.

What these three examples have in common is that the spiritual director has the role of a 'savior'. The directee needs insight, perspective, or solutions, which the director provides, drawing from life experience, intuition, or sensitive-prophetic gifting. Yet in an Ignatian perspective, the director's role is a more modest one. The insight, perspective, and solutions should come from the direct relationship between the Creator and the creature. This is the reason why the heart of spiritual direction is focused, in an Ignatian perspective, on having a conversation about God. The director doesn't 'save', rather, she thematises what is going on in the soul of the directee.

Perhaps the image of looking for gold can help illustrate this. Janet Ruffing uses this metaphor in her book on spiritual direction.[56] The director and directee together look at all the bits that pass through the gold pan: water, stones, small branches, tiny fish, sand. Everything receives a bit of attention, until you come across something that appears to be gold. Now action is needed: we found gold! In other words, the director helps the directee to notice what is happening until something comes up which seems worth a closer look.[57]

According to this image, the spiritual director searches for glimmers of gentleness, depth, simplicity, dedication, wisdom, forgiveness, warmth. While Pete gives Maria the opportunity to calmly put words to her doubts, he looks for nuggets of gold. Where does the soul shine? Where does God appear? Where does he perceive insight, clarity, simplicity, or forgiveness? In what follows, I will elaborate how this works concretely with the help of three possible scenarios. The first example is a simple and successful case: finding gold is easy. Yet in some cases, it is not easy to get access to the inner world (case 2), or the inner world may be overshadowed by darkness (case 3); in such cases, how can we dig for gold?

---

56   See Ruffing, *Spiritual Direction*, p. 57.
57   For more on this, see the helpful chapter by Barry and Connolly, 'Helping a Person Notice and Share with God Key Interior Facts', in *The Practice of Spiritual Direction*, pp. 67-83.

Case 1: Finding Gold is Easy

Imagine the following situation. John, a recent graduate of secondary school, is doing a service year in L'Arche. He comes to visit Paul, a Jesuit priest, for spiritual accompaniment. After some small talk, Paul tries to steer the conversation towards deeper waters, when John honestly admits that he does not really know what spiritual accompaniment is; he is here upon the recommendation of his supervisor at L'Arche.

J: So that's how I ended up coming to you.
P: No problem! Welcome, John.
J: Thanks. So you're going to have to tell me a bit how this works.
P: Well, why don't you tell me a bit about your journey up to this point and how you ended up where you are at.

At this point, John talks about his time in secondary school. In conclusion, he says:

J: I just need a break from school. The sister of one of my good friends is disabled. She can barely speak and needs help for everything. When I look at her, I think: what is the point of all of these studies? There is so much more.
P: (*hums in affirmation*)
J: Lately, I've noticed that when I came to visit, I was coming less for my friend and more for her. The atmosphere in that house is so unique. When I said this to my parents, along with my hesitations to go directly to college, they immediately began to talk about the L'Arche community. That's how I ended up here.

Notice that everything John is saying has something to do with the soul: his experience of the limitations of study in light of a disability, the richness of the atmosphere at his friend's house. There is a chance that each of these things is a nugget of gold, yet so far you have only touched the surface. A useful strategy therefore is to accompany John by means of active listening in revisiting his story. Probably John will further develop his story. That helps you to locate the gold that needs further exploration. There is no rush.

> P: Ah ok, so you when you visit your friend's place and meet his sister, something happens. It relativises the 'ordinary things' like studying and getting good grades.
> J: Yeah. I'm a pretty good student. I like getting good grades, but somehow that does not matter anymore. It's almost like something has broken through – something more important. Like love and care.
> P: Love and care.
> J: Yeah, as if the sunlight of love and care scatters the foggy mist of grades, studying, and wanting to become 'somebody'. (*pauses for a few moments*) I'm happy that my parents get what I mean. Some of my friends tell me that I'm wasting my life to be here in L'Arche. Luckily my parents aren't saying that.

Notice that the method of actively listening really works here. John specifies love, care, and sunlight. After using the captivating image of sunlight and mist – an image which evokes the world of his soul – he also mentions his parents. At this point, Paul will probably gently move along with him and talk about his parents, yet later he should return to the themes of love, care, and sunlight. Can John say more about these things?

In this case, looking for gold turned out to be easy. John's transparency makes it clear where Paul has to look. The gold lies directly on the surface, even though John can still grow in his familiarity with his own soul and in his ability to put his experience into words – something suggested by the fact that he moves from talking about the light of his soul to talking about his parents. If Paul were to invite him to refocus on his soul, that will probably be enough to get him back on track. And even if this doesn't work, Paul can still consider this conversation to have been successful: together they have seen something shining within John's soul and examined it a bit.

Case 2: Finding Gold is Difficult

However, what if the gold is much more hidden? How should you proceed when the directee reveals only a few things about what is going on in his soul? Imagine, for example, that during the second meeting with Paul, John gives a general report about what he's been up to and what's happening in the community, rather than anything about his soul. Such a conversation can progress as follows:

P: Welcome, John. Nice to see you again.

After some small talk about the weather, his commute, or other such things, Paul tries to get down to business.

P: And how's it going at L'Arche now that the first few weeks are over?

J: I'm still happy. Every morning we have a short prayer service. I always try to get there a little bit early so that I can pray a bit on my own. Afterwards, we all have breakfast together. It's always a bit rushed because everybody needs to get to work or another appointment on time. After the service, I have a little free time until my housemates return. Once they are back home, I need to help with preparing tea and cooking food. I've never had to cook at home, so I've had to learn a few things.

P: So every morning, the first thing you do is pray and eat breakfast, and later on around noon you meet up again with your housemates and cook together?

J: Yeah, I cook twice a week. On Wednesday evenings we have

a spiritual evening. I take part in a book club together with a few people from the neighbourhood. We're reading a book by Henri Nouwen called *The Return of the Prodigal Son*. Nouwen really has a wonderful explanation of that Bible story. I just recently had a conversation about this with my pastor – and he had quite a few things to say about this too!

Notice that John is telling Paul anything and everything about his life in the community: the daily rhythm, the cooking, the weekly evening of reflection. His experiences are barely touched at this point. Paul receives a lot of information about what John is busy doing rather than about what is going on in his soul. Therefore, Paul should search a way to connect with the deeper layer. Paul may do so as follows:

P: It's nice to know what your days look like. May I ask how you are feeling? What is it like to live in L'Arche?

J: Oh, it's great. I mean, I really feel like this is the place for me. The other residents are all very nice to me, and I feel accepted in the group. On top of that, I've learned how to cook!

P: And how about your housemates? How has that been?

J: Umm…yeah … I needed some time to get used to living with people with disabilities. Sometimes you really have to have a lot of patience!

P: I see. Patience.

J: Yeah…patience. Honestly, that is something that I struggle with.

P: The last time we met, we talked about how you ended up in L'Arche. You said something about the atmosphere in the family of a friend who has a sister with a disability. Do you still remember what you said?

J: Yeah, definitely! (*puts on a big smile*) We talked about the atmosphere at their house. Right? That's what you mean?

P: That sounded like your original inspiration for joining L'Arche. Do you still have that inspiration? Or is it now difficult to have patience?

J: That's a good question. Sometimes that inspiration seems gone, really. I haven't been sleeping well. Sometimes my housemates get agitated at night and we need to help them to calm down. At the moment I'm quite tired. And then I also need to be patient ... *(pauses for a moment)* Yeah, honestly, I kinda forgot what brought me to L'Arche in the first place.

P: Ok, so you kinda forgot it. And now?

J: It seems to be coming back a little bit: the richness I felt at my friend's house, the simplicity, the warmth, the light. *(laughs)* Ha-ha, even the patience!

Notice that Paul's first intervention is quite gentle: 'It's nice to know what your days look like. May I ask how you are feeling?' In this way, he suggests a conclusion and a shift to a different topic: how it feels. He is searching for a way in. Where is the hatch, the door that gives access to the inside? His later intervention is a stronger one: he reaches back to a strong moment of spiritual experience in the past. Can that past experience function as a means of opening that door?

This case is a good illustration of spiritual direction that does not 'take off' easily. That is not because there is no gold to be found, but because the conversation remains at the level of thoughts and events. John begins by describing his daily rhythm and then talks about Henri Nouwen's book. He hardly speaks about how things are going at L'Arche for him and what he is experiencing. The experienced director will take note that the directee lives 'in his head', at least at this moment. (By the way, there is nothing wrong with paying some attention to your head. Otherwise, how would you be able to perceive and think?)

Why do people stay at the surface? What is the reason that some people are more comfortable dealing with thoughts and facts rather than exploring the inner world of the soul? One reason, most certainly, is that talking about the soul makes us vulnerable. Personal history plays a role here: have you had, for example, a negative past experience with being vulnerable? In such a case, focusing on facts, thoughts, and events helps you to avoid such an experience. Character can also play a role: some people are more at ease speaking about personal things than others. Are you, for example, more of an introvert or an extrovert? A 'tough guy' who is a bit of a macho will like to keep 'feelings' at a distance. Culture plays a role too, whether of a country or a particular family. In some cultures, people are more comfortable discussing art, philosophy, sports, or current events than they are sharing personal things. Lastly, it should also be noted that the culture of the Church and theology play an important role here. As I already noted in the introduction, Churches tend to be more concerned with orthodoxy and orthopraxy rather than with what happens to individuals in their hearts, minds, and consciences.

Even though it's understandable that someone may not be comfortable with talking about her soul, spiritual experience is crucial for spiritual direction. Spiritual direction cannot remain merely focused on recounting events, thoughts, or reflections. In an Ignatian perspective, what happens in the soul is an important place to find God (see Chapter 2). In their book, Barry and Connolly devote much time to what they call the spiritual director's tasks of 'fostering a contemplative attitude', an attitude which they identify as being frequently lacking in those coming to spiritual direction.[58]

In order to underscore these thoughts and to encourage spiritual directors to persist in their search for gold, I would like to refer to the concerns that Ignatius had in this regard. In one of the introductory Notes in the *Spiritual Exercises*, he instructs the spiritual director to be worried in case of an absence of inner spiritual dynamic in what the directee is sharing. When that occurs, the director must carefully enquire about the directee's spiritual life so that he can give helpful advice as to what could be done differently. In Ignatius' own words:

---

58 See Barry and Connolly, *The Practice of Spiritual Direction*, particularly the chapter 'Fostering a Contemplative Attitude', pp. 47–66.

> When the one giving the exercises notices that the exercitant is not experiencing any spiritual motions in his or her soul, such as consolations or desolations, or is not being moved one way or another by different spirits, the director should question the retreatant about the Exercises: Whether he or she is making them at the appointed times, how they are being made, and whether the Additional Directives are being diligently observed. The director should ask about each of these items in particular. (SE, no. 6)

This shows that according to Ignatius, matters of the soul were crucially important for spiritual accompaniment, and furthermore, it also suggests that inner movements of the soul are not the privilege of only a few select 'spiritual masters' but accessible for all. That is true for a retreat and likewise for everyday life.

If the thematising of the soul is not progressing smoothly, as was the case with John, then you just have to keep at it. As you have good reasons, you must persist in trying to find a way to talk about matters of the soul. In spite of your determination, you may not see many results, or not soon in any case. It is not as if John will immediately open up once you ask him something about his soul. As the cultivation of the soul is long and hard work, you have to always engage in this in a gentle and unrushed manner, without using force. There is no guarantee of success. Sometimes you will hit the mark; sometimes it will not work.

Gentleness is of the utmost importance. A director who is too persistent will shoot herself in the foot. John will not understand why you are pushing him to talk about the soul. This will make him feel either ganged up on, or make him feel like a screw-up. Consequently, he will not trust you and will resist this type of conversation. Instead, always take it easy and keep it light. A small story or joke can be quite appropriate.

Concretely you can start simply with the material that is out on the table. For example, John was able to say something about the good experience he had at his friend's house. Why don't you start by revisiting that and trying to deepen it? You could, for example, invite John to again connect with those experiences. What made that experience in the past so agreeable? You could also draw a connection between that experience and the present reality – which is exactly what Paul did in the case above. 'Ok, so you kinda forgot it. And now?' That is a first step. The idea here is that later on, John will be able to perceive and describe more subtle spiritual movements, such as in his daily life in L'Arche, while vacuuming the living room or patiently peeling potatoes with his housemates.

I will discuss the various ways you can help John make better contact with his experiences more thoroughly in the following chapter. By way of conclusion, it might be good to point out that, up to this point, I have been assuming that directees are healthy and balanced people. If your efforts continue to bear very little fruit and you are unable to make contact with someone's inner world, that may well indicate that there is a mental block of one kind or another. It would probably be a good idea, at this point, to seek the professional assistance of a psychologist. While spirituality can play an assisting and supporting role, spiritual direction is no substitute for other kinds of professional attention.

Case 3: Finding Gold amid Darkness

Until this point, the greatest hindrance to finding gold was the directee's shyness. Possibly he is uneasy or unaccustomed to speaking about matters of the soul. There can, however, be another obstruction: when everything appears to be dark. Any possible light is overshadowed and suffocated by darkness, confusion, lack of clarity, heaviness; these themes absorb all the attention of the directee. What do you do then? If you take these experiences seriously, which seems commendable, how can you avoid 'therapeutic seduction' (see Chapter 2)? How do you ensure that you do not end up on the slippery slope which leads to only more darkness and heaviness?

Take, for example, Samantha, who feels depressed. Her grandmother has just died – a grandmother who was really a second mother to her (if not really her 'first' one). She always felt at ease when her grandmother was around. In addition, Samantha has been struggling with feelings of a more general sadness lately. Her studies are not going well, her friends don't have much time for her, and her prayer life is so dry that she has recently given up on it. With all of these things going on, she comes to see you.

In such instances, it is very important that the spiritual director continues to believe that somewhere there is light or hope, against all odds, even if the directee cannot tell you where it might be. Like the detectives from the cartoons – picture a man with a bowler hat on his head, slightly bent over, with a magnifying glass in his hand – you search for clues, using the material that is available. In this case, the 'material at hand' for the director-detective is Samantha's story as she relates it, apparently without any glimmers of light. Anything and everything that is related in the story, the detective scrutinises. Is there anything further, anything deeper, in what you have been told? Do you notice anything that is worth investigation, where you suspect there may be light or hope? With questions like these in the back of your mind, you go along with the directee's feelings of depression and sadness, but you don't let these feelings entice you. You remain committed to 'the plan': to search for gold.

Sometimes it is sufficient to walk alongside the directee while she relates her arduous journey. By mirroring the darkness and heaviness, you bring the directee some relief. Slowly she settles down, and light breaks through the cracks. That is what we already saw with Jack the theology student in Chapter 4. By going along with his story and concluding that you yourself can imagine why he would want to stop his studies, you prompted Jack to discover: 'But I don't want to stop!' Jack ceased to be focused on only the things that have not been going well; suddenly he came in contact with the original moment of inspiration again. Another typical example is somebody who is sick. When you abstain from consoling and pious cheering up, but simply allow the patient to share the story of diagnoses, doctors, and despair, there is a fair chance that the patient will at some point say, 'But the nurses here are really kind'.

Sometimes, however, the darkness remains. Let's say that that is how things are with Samantha. How should you respond to persistent darkness? How can you be a good detective? One possibility would be to react in the following way:

P: Wow, Samantha that is quite a story. So many difficult experiences: your studies aren't going well, the situation with your friends, the death of your grandmother. And to make matters worse, God is remaining silent.
S: Yeah it's been really difficult.
P: So everything started with your studies which weren't going well. Was this because of some bad grades you received, or were your classes not really interesting anymore?
S: Hmm... I actually wouldn't know. It just isn't working anymore.
P: So you get out of bed and you immediately think: gosh, I just don't want to go to class today. Something like that?
S: Yeah something like that. Pff... I think so, at least.
P: 'Pff'?
S: Yeah, pff...

In this short conversation, three things deserve our attention. First of all, note that you begin by accepting Samantha's story by summarily mirroring it back to her. For Samantha this must be comforting. Where else can Samantha meet someone who just listens to her story without immediately trying to jump in and 'help'? In Chapter 4 I suggested that listening and accepting is God's first response to us, and perhaps the most important one. That you do this for her as well is already a balm for her soul. Possibly, the experience of being accepted will be her first little bit of gold.

The second thing to note is that Samantha's reaction to seeing herself in the mirror is very different from Jack's. Whereas Jack cried out in protest, 'I don't want to stop', Samantha readily agrees that things are very difficult for her and stops there: 'Yeah it's been really difficult'. In this case, it's your job to closely examine each experience in order to see what lies at the core of each of them. Is there, in one of these experiences, a small glimmer of light? It's usually best to start at the beginning. Resist the temptation to immediately opt for a 'pious' theme. While there is a high likelihood that something is going on around her prayer life, it seems better if you also explore the other issues that she brought up: her studies, friends, and her experience in prayer. (Think of the instruction to 'take it easy' from Chapter 3.)

Thirdly, note that you are working hard. Samantha is not readily opening up to you and she gives you the impression that she really doesn't want to talk about this. Each answer is very short and to the point. She doesn't go to any deeper level, evidenced by her answers of 'Hmm, I actually wouldn't know' and 'Yeah, something like that'.

Nevertheless, you are to stay patient and gentle. You do this by continuing to talk about the things she brings up. At this point, something small happens because she agrees with the 'Pff' that the spiritual director proposes. Generally speaking, however, she barely reacts. The burden to carry on the conversation is clearly on you. In what follows, I offer an example as to how you may deal with this. It is meant to illustrate how you can be tenacious without making things too heavy and overbearing.

P: What does that 'pff' mean? Are you tired or bored? Just like the sigh that you make before you leave your dorm to go to class as you force yourself to open the door and go down the stairs? Or is it a sign that you are overloaded: it's too difficult and you just can't do it anymore? Or is there more to it than that?

S: Yeah… I really wish I knew. (*takes a moment of silence*) Maybe what I'm feeling is mostly a sense of tiredness … I'm just feeling worn out. I feel like all I have to do is record more and more information: facts, methods,

history ... always more and more.
P: So as soon as you start studying it begins: a feeling that you are under fire from all of this information. Like this, almost *(he pretends that he is under fire and dodging bullets)*. You're not dodging bullets, but facts, methods, and history. These are the things that are being fired upon you and it's all too much.
S: Yes, it really is all too much. I can't handle it anymore. All I want is some rest.
P: Rest.
S: Yes, rest. Enough that I can go hide for a little while. A little while without information, without being bothered. A little bit of rest.

Here it seems as if all of your efforts are starting to bear some fruit. Just as in the examples from the first intervention with Paul, we appear to be getting somewhere. The director has succeeded and can now rejoice over the result. Note that towards the end of this short dialogue, Samantha is actually speaking longer than the director; she has started to speak! She succeeds in identifying what burdens her. By means of the word 'tiredness' and the image of being 'under fire' she admits that things are all 'too much' and that she desires 'rest'.

Possibly more could be said, but this is definitely a promising beginning. The elusive and impenetrable darkness starts to take some shape and form. Moreover, there is some insight into what is missing: rest. Someone who is trained in Ignatian spirituality will immediately think of the term 'desire', but it's not necessarily the right time to dwell on this. It's enough to think back to the detective who, with his quizzical look, was searching for clues. Samantha's desire for rest is a clue. While it's true that you have not yet uncovered the fullness of the light – her desire for rest indicates that she does not yet have it – you seem to have discovered the starting point of a way that leads to the light. At this point, it begins to gently glimmer.

Thus, the conversation with Samantha illustrates that there are various possibilities to find light. After it became distantly perceivable – so you hope – through the experience of being accepted, it begins now to shine a bit because you've helped her identify what is really at the root of her experience and because of the hopeful perspective that brings. It is this perspective that you can build on in future sessions.

With regard to the temptation to be 'therapeutic', I suggest the following. Earlier, I proposed that the director must not be tempted by a fascination for the darkness. Consequently, she should remain interested in finding the light (see Chapter 2). Nevertheless, Samantha's story shows that you can't simply ignore the darkness. If you do that, you're not accepting Samantha as she is. Perhaps the first glimmer of light is to be found by accepting the darkness. What I am advocating is approaching the darkness in such a way that the light within it can appear. Furthermore, it is also possible and sometimes necessary to evaluate the heaviness and burdens that are mentioned by means of discernment or their reference to God (see Chapter 7).

Conclusion

This chapter has offered a first step toward what I would identify as the core of spiritual direction: having a conversation about spiritual experiences and about the soul. We have seen that it is important to be attentive to the things that glimmer and shine. At the same time, this chapter is anything but fully complete: it is full of loose ends. What do you do, for example, once you've found the gold? How can you enter into a conversation about that? What are the tools for doing this well? Moreover, how do you know whether or not the thing that is shining really is gold? The attraction to do a service year at L'Arche that John experiences can, after all, be impure. Is he idealising his friend's family? Or is he, perhaps, avoiding his studies, something that he likes a lot less recently? And who knows, maybe Samantha's dream about wanting more rest is only an illusion? In other words: what do you do once you've identified something that you think is gold? In the next chapters, I hope to answer that question.

6: FOURTH TOOL

GOING DEEPER

The last chapter addressed how one should search for the thing which shines. By this, we've made an inroad toward what is the very heart of spiritual accompaniment. The next step is to go deeper. After you have identified the shiny golden object in your sifter, you examine and admire it. Just like when visiting a museum, you pause in front of the painting that appeals to you in order to take a closer look at it and absorb yourself in it. It is not enough only to take note of the fact that this painting is there or that it is beautiful. You pause in admiration, determining what about it precisely appeals to you, and allowing yourself to be absorbed by it. Another example could be when you go and visit a newborn baby. You don't just observe that 'this is a baby', but you also really pay attention to all of the little details: the round little ears, the cute nose, the thin fingers. 'What a beautiful baby!'

It works the same in spiritual accompaniment, except that you don't admire a painting or a baby, but rather somebody's God-given spiritual experience. Earlier, I noted that God makes use of such experiences in order to confirm a person on his life journey. It's really a gift. Wouldn't this make it worthwhile, almost a moral duty, to pay special attention to these experiences and to specify what the gift precisely is?

Before I go on to present various ways to engage in this process of going deeper, I'd like to first present an example of the fruit of such a process. After this I will present five possible deepening interventions. I conclude with a couple of general comments on restraint, determination, the usefulness of closed questions, and the temptation of the directee to hide himself.

It is, of course, important to note that a conversation seldomly proceeds in a linear manner. It is not that listening is followed by searching for gold, which in turn is followed by deepening, without returning to earlier tools. The linear presentation outlined in this book is a pedagogical tool only. Spiritual accompaniment is really a dynamic process wherein you constantly search for gold, constantly strive after relaxation, and constantly engage in active listening.

The Fruit of Going Deeper

So first of all, let's highlight the fruit of the process of going deeper. Earlier we met Esther, a mother of three children and the chief of staff in a regional hospital. She related to the pastoral worker Renata the energy that she feels and the things she was thankful for (Chapter 3). Renata then pursued those themes further with Esther. Because this conversation is a good example of the fruits of a deepened conversation, I repeat it here along with some commentary, from the moment that Renata summarises what Esther has related with regard to having energy.

> R: So many things happening, Esther! (*with a smile*) You're busy!
>
> E: Yeah, indeed. I feel a lot of energy. At the end of the day I am tired, so I go to bed on time; the next day I get up refreshed. (*quiet for a moment*) I am so ... well, I guess, so happy to have so much energy.
>
> R: You have a lot of energy and you are happy with that.
>
> E: Yes. In fact, if I can be honest with you, I consider it a special grace. I feel strong, I can do a lot: my work, taking care of the children, everything.
>
> R: Yes, I'm impressed that you do so much! And you said (*pauses for a moment*) that you consider it a grace?

E: Um, yeah. (*quiet for a moment*) I mean I see it as a gift. I strongly feel that I don't just do it myself. I'm given strength; I receive it.

Up until now the conversation has been easy going. Renata mirrors and Esther responds by adding more information. She consistently goes deeper. Notice that you don't need to rush; all you have to do is to calmly note that you've heard what Esther said.

Also notice that you don't resort to impersonal coldness but instead share that you're impressed by all of the things which Esther manages to accomplish. Some people maintain that you should refrain from saying such appreciative things and instead remain neutral. By making comments like this, they maintain, you could be seen as passing a judgment; your approval may provoke patterns of desired behavior. While that would indeed be regrettable, being overly distant and maintaining a fabricated impersonal neutrality are just as undesirable.

Finally, notice that in the meantime other things have come to the surface: energy, grace, gift, and receiving.

Then, Renata decides on a stronger intervention: she asks Esther to identify what kind of experience these things are. This is a typical question to go deeper. As Renata strongly gets the impression that the experience of receiving has more depth to it, that is where she puts the spade in the ground. Renata in fact pauses the conversation: 'Let's not pursue talking about the many things that you do or about your situation at home; instead, let's zoom in'. That is her agenda when she asks, 'What kind of experience is that "receiving" you just spoke of?' As we saw in Chapter 3, the conversation continues thus:

E: What a beautiful question! It's a bit like a friend coming by unexpectedly, and then we have coffee and cake in the garden, and everything is well.
R: So you're unexpectedly catching up, in the garden, and then things are well.
E: Yes, that's how it is.

Fourth Tool: Going Deeper 79

R: And when things are well, what happens? What do you feel?

E: It's very still and very overwhelming at the same time. This unexpected encounter was really nice. It brought some sort of a calm peace. Yet it was overwhelming too, because in all its simpleness it was so rich. It's like finding flowers everywhere: in the kitchen, in the living room, at work, in the bedroom, on the stairs. Almost too good to be true.

R: So when you say that your energy is a gift, a grace, that it's like someone who comes to visit, and things are well.

E: Yes, after such a meeting I feel very energetic again, very rich. (*smiles*) Then I can take on the world again!

R: (*with a smile*) And from what I'm hearing, that's exactly what you do, take on the world! (*pauses*) Does God have something to do with that energy, with that experience?

E: Well, I think so. But I'm not totally sure. It's not as if I see a Jesus-figure in a white robe, speaking to me.

R: So there's no Jesus-figure?

E: No.

R: And no God either, really?

E: Well, maybe God. I feel that the energy I receive is caring and loving. I can do a lot of good with it. I think I see something of God in that.

The short dialogue demonstrates the beneficial fruit of deepening the conversation. Renata's inviting questions brings Esther to the image of a friend who comes to visit. By means of another deepening question, Renata brings Esther to elaborate on the word 'meeting': feeling at home, being at ease, as well as the new image of bouquets of flowers. This is the very heart of spiritual accompaniment. At this point, the conversation addresses what is moving deep within Esther's heart. This is nothing short of a revealing conversation; through it, Esther seeks and finds news words to express her experience. She had already sensed that there was something beautiful going on here; she's now able to name and specify it.

Yet how can you do this? What possibilities are there to pause the conversation in order to go deeper? What can you say as a spiritual director to accomplish this sort of deepening? In what follows, I present a couple of possible 'types' of deepening interventions: 1) exploring experience and feeling, 2) exploring images, 3) making things concrete, 4) making things broad, and 5) exploring fruits. In each case, I illustrate how it works with the help of an example. These examples show time and again how beneficial deepening interventions can be.

Deepening Interventions 1: Exploring Experience and Feeling
The example of Esther and Renata illustrated a first 'type' of deepening intervention: the question about experience or feeling. You could also use this intervention in the case of John, a young seminarian who is having his very first experiences of spiritual accompaniment. He is quite new to it all and that means that you will have to negotiate the speed with which you steer towards deeper waters. In this case, while it's clear that something is shining, it's less clear what exactly John is experiencing. By asking John to speak of his feeling or experience, you can help him to come to a moment of deepening. Before I show how that works, let me lay out the scenario, illustrated here in a conversation between John and his spiritual director, Paul.

P: Welcome, John.
J: Thanks. So, you're going to have to tell me about how all of this is supposed to work.
P: Ok, so why don't we start by you telling me how your journey has brought you to this point.
J: Well, I've always been an altar server, and I've always enjoyed being in church.
P: Hmm.

Fourth Tool: Going Deeper

J: I really can't fully explain it. The seminary president always asked me what that feeling of enjoyment actually was, but I could never answer him. I can only say that once I went to confession with a retired pastor, and that was really a unique experience. As I was riding my bike home, I had this thought that I would like to become a priest too. And that's how I ended up here, I guess.

P: Alright then. So first you noticed that it was enjoyable to be in church. But the drop that caused the cup to overflow was that special meeting with the pastor.

J: Yes. He spoke about God's mercy, and that gave me so much hope and light that I thought, I would also like to be a priest.

P: Hope and light.

Up until now, Paul's interventions have been rather gentle. First, he hummed 'hmm', afterwards he summarised what John had said, and finally he astutely mirrored back 'hope and light'. Although there is much to look at here, it seems that it is still a bit too early for Paul to pose a deepening question. After all, Paul and John barely know each other. It could be better to keep things a bit general and remain talking about the concrete things John has done. What was his favorite job as an altar server? Did he serve Mass each week, or only once a month? Did he serve alone? What did the church where he served look like? It seems wise to go easy in this way rather than jumping immediately into the deep end (see Chapter 3). Meanwhile, you must remember the rich language that John used: 'hope and light'.

After you've spent some time talking about general things, and once you feel that there is a bit of trust between you, then you can begin to go a bit deeper. Such a deepening can unfold as follows:

P: John, earlier in our conversation you said that you always enjoyed being in church; you couldn't really explain it, but it was still quite important. Would you mind if we go back and

>   look at that a bit further?
> J: Oh ok. Yeah, I can try that.
> P: Would you be able to describe how you experience being in church?
> J: Umm ... it's nice. I think it's enjoyable.
> P: So it's an enjoyable experience.
> J: Yeah ... or is it not good that I say that?

In this dialogue, you're slowly but surely heading towards the moment of deepening. First, you extended a friendly invitation to John to engage in this, to which he responded that he was willing to try it. Then you engaged in a first deepening intervention by asking him to describe his experience. This is the same kind of intervention which Renata did with Esther: 'What are you experiencing?' You could have also asked about what he felt, or the kinds of images which his experience brought to the surface.

Whereas Esther seemed quite comfortable with that question, John seems a bit unsure of himself. It's difficult for him to find words to describe his experience. The best he's able to come up with is 'nice' or 'enjoyable'. It's going roughly. (You may compare this to what I said in the previous chapter under the heading 'Finding Gold is Difficult'). You could continue to pursue the same route by, for example, inviting John to say more about the other items he brought into the conversation: his experience of confessing to the retired pastor, or 'hope and light'. Perhaps that would work, but chances are that it would not be all that successful. It seems you might need a few other skills (other than patience) in order to get further with John. Luckily, there are, indeed, other types of deepening interventions at your disposal.

Deepening Interventions 2: Exploring Images

Another helpful approach works with images or representations. The spiritual director invites the directee to go deeper by thematising the various images that have been mentioned or by searching for images. This type of deepening interventions is based on the supposition that

Fourth Tool: Going Deeper

people articulate their experiences not only through words or feelings but also by means of images and representations.

The example of Esther and Renata recounted at the beginning of this chapter illustrates this well. Renata said: 'What kind of experience is that "receiving" you just spoke of?' Esther responded: 'What a beautiful question! It's a bit like a friend coming by unexpectedly, and then we have coffee and cake in the garden, and everything is well'. In this case, Esther provided an image herself. While Renata asked about a feeling, Esther made use if an image in her answer. It's as if she said: 'In order to provide some depth to my experience of receiving, it's best if I make use of an image: it's like an unexpected visit from a friend'. This example illustrates that images and representations can be helpful in the process of providing some depth to spiritual experiences.

This example also suggests that directors have to remain flexible. The more extensive the director's treasury of deepening interventions is, the easier it becomes to offer something useful to the specific directee whom he is accompanying. Sometimes, this requires that the director takes the initiative to invite the directee on a certain path. 'Is there perhaps a meaningful image that captures the event, the experience that you just shared?' Sometimes, the directee will come up with an image, as was the case with Esther. Regardless of the directee's exact description, a director should be highly attentive when a directee makes use of an image. Because of their power and potential for deepening, images must be explored. Here are two helpful examples to illustrate what I mean:

> R: So it's like having an unexpected visit with a friend over coffee and cake while sitting in the garden. What a lovely image!
> E: Yeah, I imagine that we just go and sit there together. It feels so unforced ... spontaneous even.
> R: I see: unforced, spontaneous. So that's what the unexpected coffee and cake in your garden mean.
> E: Yes. It's similar to when you receive an unexpected bouquet

>   of flowers and wonder, 'What did I do to deserve this?' It's a gift.
> R: (*Smiling*) There is that image of a gift again!
> E: Haha, yes there is that gift again.

Note what the director is doing and the kind of effect that it has on the directee. Renata stops briefly at the image of the coffee in the garden by mirroring it back to Esther. Admittedly the deepening effect of this is relatively limited; it gives some results, but not many. You quickly find yourself back to that image of the gift. (By the way, that is perfectly fine.) Notice as well that it is easy to make a light joke about that.

How do you go on from this point? You could now try to use other kinds of interventions in order to go a bit deeper. Perhaps a question concerning her feelings would work. There is indeed a chance that such a question would lead toward another image insofar as the 'ground' has been aerated a bit. If this type of deepening intervention does not work, maybe one of the next ones that we have yet to discuss might prove to be successful. After all, Esther's use of the word 'grace' suggests a transcendent or religious dimension.

In other cases, following up an image will turn out to be very powerful. With every further step you take you enter more deeply into the world of the directee's imagination; this comes with stunning effects that are close to revelation. The way to do so is by 'simply' using active listening – or listening and following, as I prefer – to accompany the directee while she unpacks the image. By 'naively' and uncritically asking her what her world actually looks like and what happens in that world, the director does the directee a great service.

The following case-study illustrates how this works. Imagine two Benedictine monks, one a novice, the other his novice master. They are having a conversation about prayer.

> N: You know what I've really been enjoying lately? Simply going for a walk in the garden! I know it sounds a bit silly. My prayer life has been so dry lately… it's really been a

Fourth Tool: Going Deeper

        struggle to keep at it because when I pray it seems like it lasts an eternity without giving me anything in return. My evening walk, on the other hand, is extremely pleasant.

NM: That evening walk is good for you.

N: Yes. It's nearly dusk, the blackbird sings gently, and the wind is soft. It is just so relaxing. Life-giving and relaxing.

NM: Life-giving and relaxing.

N: Yes. I have this feeling that 'this is good'. Sometimes I go and have a seat on a bench overlooking the meadows, and it's almost as if God himself comes near to me. As if we are sitting together on that bench.

NM: Sitting together with God on a bench ... (*moment of silence*)

N: Yes.

NM: And is he sitting there already when you arrive? Or does he show up later?

N: It's as if we had been walking together and then he suggests that we have a seat. It's almost like he says: 'Is it alright with you that I sit here next to you?' (*smiles*) A bit like he's saying, 'Scoot over so I can fit there too!'

NM: So, he asks you to scoot over so that he can have a seat as well.

N: Yes, that's what he says. Well, alright I don't know if he really says that so much as I feel it. Perhaps it's better described as being a soft glance rather than something with words. He looks at me calmly.

NM: And as you're sitting there with him, how does that go? Do you converse? Are you looking at each other?

N: (*smiles*) You want to know what we do? It's as if he leans up against me a bit and I against him. Just like you would do with a good friend: shoulder to shoulder.

Note that the novice master doesn't choose to focus on the novice's dry prayer life but, rather, on his routine of making an evening walk. He doesn't opt for the obviously 'pious' theme of prayer, nor does he give into the 'therapeutic seduction' of focusing on the 'problem'. The novice master chooses instead the topic wherein there is clearly the most life: the evening walk. This is an example of one of the core values of spiritual direction, namely, giving preference to the things which lead to life (Chapter 2). Nevertheless, it can also, of course, sometimes be good to explore the dryness of the directee's prayer life.

Also notice that the novice master goes along with the images brought up by the directee, enquiring in great detail what happened with this 'sitting together with God on a bench' and how it worked. He could have gone in another direction. For example, he could have asked him to describe further the feeling of 'life-giving and relaxing'. He preferred instead to unpack the image.

It's possible that this deepening seems a bit weird. Is it really a good idea to engage in fantasy during something as serious as spiritual accompaniment? Aren't we grown ups? If you try this, however, you will quickly discover how powerful and revelatory this way of proceeding is. As a matter of fact, you have just witnessed how the novice master's interest in the details of the novice's image have transformed a story of a pleasant evening walk into a personal testimony about a very intimate encounter with God. This may convince you to leave behind your hesitations.

Deepening Interventions 3: Making Things Concrete

In the search for the depths, one is generally inclined to focus on the inner-personal dimension. One looks for what happens 'within', for example, when a person indicates that his soul expands, brings up an image that seems to be meaningful, or shares an experience of peace or gentleness, and so forth. However, sometimes depth is to be found just as much in the world around. Another kind of intervention, then, focuses not on the inner dimensions but, rather, on concrete things 'out there'. After all, spiritual experiences occur in concrete circumstances.

Fourth Tool: Going Deeper

It can be helpful to make things concrete and thereby deepen spiritual experience.

By making things concrete I mean that you accompany the directee to the place where her good experience took place. Admittedly, that does not touch the depth of the experience directly, but it still brings the directee in contact with the experience and invites her to explore it further. In that sense, it counts as a deepening intervention. At a later stage, concretising can maybe form the basis for thematising spiritual experience in a more direct way.[59]

Concretising is an important asset to the toolbox of deepening interventions, that is useful for people who are less at ease with what is going on 'within', as seems to be the case for John, the young seminarian. For him, this would probably work better than directly asking about feelings or images. He doesn't seem very comfortable in talking about these things. With this in mind, let's take a look at how concretising works with the help of the following example.

[handwritten annotation: fill in some details]

P: Ah ok, so it's a pleasant experience. Can you say something as to how that happens concretely? I'm imagining a Sunday morning and you getting on your bike to head to church. Maybe your parents go with you, maybe not. And then you think: wonderful, this is really nice. Something like that?

J: Yes. Actually, it begins already on the evening before. Then I think to myself: tomorrow I can go to church again! I get my dress shirt ready and polish my shoes.

P: Wow, you really prepare yourself! And your pleasant feeling begins then already?

J: Yeah, sometimes it does, but not always. Sometimes the feeling doesn't surface until I come into the church. It's really a lovely old church – Gothic, I think. I always arrive

---

[59] In a way this resembles the 'Composition of Place', one of the characteristic elements of Ignatian Scripture meditation. In the Composition of Place, the retreatant is invited to image a certain Scripture passage as concretely as possible, for example, how Jesus enters Jericho and meets Zaccheus. Is the city small or big? How is Zaccheus dressed and how does he manage to climb the tree? What do people say? How does Jesus look? Imagining a story and bringing it alive in this way – as if it was a movie – can facilitate deep spiritual encounters with God.

early, so it's usually pretty quiet when I go inside. It's just so pleasant, the silence of that building. It is almost as if the silence welcomes me.

Here you can see how this process of concretising works: John's general comment that it was 'pleasant' now develops contours. It seems that this feeling begins on Saturday evening as he gets his clothes ready for Sunday morning and also on Sunday morning before the start of the Mass. This deepening could be further enhanced by, for example, zooming in on one of these moments. (As it could be by asking if there are other words than 'pleasant', which seems a bit superficial.) But remember that John is only at the beginning of his spiritual journey, so maybe it's better if you take it easy. Therefore, why not allow John the possibility of further elaborating on his experience? Are there other pleasant moments?

P: So, it's pleasant to prepare yourself for the Mass, and also pleasant to spend time in the quiet church beforehand. What about the Mass itself? Is that also a pleasant experience?

J: Oh definitely. My favorite thing to do as a server is to be the thurifer. It's so nice to process into the church swinging the thurible. It makes me feel that this is a holy place. That I can serve in such a capacity, that we are gathered there to give glory to God ... that's a special feeling.

You can continue with him for a while in such a fashion. The fruit of this process is clear: John's comment that it was 'pleasant' has become concrete and specific. It seems to have something to do with his preparations, the silent moments before the beginning of Mass, and incense.

Deepening Interventions 4: Making Things Broader

How can you proceed further with John? After all, while you can concretise things for some time, eventually there comes a moment when you've done that enough. What do you do then? Certainly, you could immediately go back to the domain of John's interiority with questions about his experience and feeling, but this would probably only serve to torment him. For this reason, it could be better to remain with the external domain and to use another, related type of deepening intervention: making things broader.

This intervention is related to the previous one ('Making Things Concrete'). Here also, the orientation is outward rather than inward. But whereas in concretising the director asks the directee about the concrete details of what he has brought up, here the director charts a new course. The director invites the directee to consider whether or not the experience he has been relating occurs also in other contexts. You could, for example, ask John if he experiences the same pleasant feelings at other times. Is it strictly connected to the context of Mass, or does he also feel this at other moments? This exchange could proceed as follows:

P: Lovely, John, I am happy to get a sense of how connected you are to the church, and how that is a pleasant experience for you. You are quite lucky, I must say! I'm happy for you! (*pauses for a moment and then looks interested*) May I ask you something more? It sounds like it's a pretty rich experience from what you've told me. I'm wondering if you ever have that feeling of pleasantness at other moments. It's clearly connected to the things that you do in church, but do you ever feel it at other moments?

J: What do you mean?

P: Well, for example when you pray Evening Prayer alone in your room? Or when you're on your bike headed to class? Or, maybe, when you're having a conversation with a good friend? Do you have a similarly pleasant feeling at such times as well?

In this bit of dialogue, Paul is much more talkative than directors usually should be. You might think that he is somewhat overdoing it. However, in practice this is really not the case. Paul introduces a new perspective and explains what he means. When you're introducing something new, it's more than appropriate to take some time to familiarise the directee with what you're aiming at. John's reaction ('What do you mean?') confirms that you were not going too slowly. The goal of using examples in your explanation is to help. It's not that you are putting words into someone's mouth so much as you are in a helpful way giving the directee a feeling for the sorts of things that you mean.

The conversation in this example can go forward in a variety of ways. I'll provide two possibilities.

J: Yeah, now that you ask me, it makes me think ... yes, I have felt it at other moments. It might sound a bit crazy, but I have the same feeling when I go running. Most of the time I really don't feel like going. When I lived at home, my mom would always say to me: 'Come on John, it's good for your health'. I can still hear her voice ... (*smiles*) ... my mom moved here with me! But once I get back to the house and have a shower, I feel reborn. I really didn't want to run, yet when I do, it works out well. That's a really pleasant feeling, too.

P: Huh, well see that's good. So the pleasant feeling is not only something which comes up when you're busy with 'holy' things, but also when you're doing something as mundane as going for a run. (*pauses for a moment, then smiles*) Maybe there are other examples ...

In this case, your question made John see more than he had seen before. It shows how broadening interventions can be quite useful. They are revelatory. You may even mirror that this is something new. In this way, you give John the chance to add something to what he said. Would he like to say something more?

Fourth Tool: Going Deeper

It is, of course, possible that John only experiences this pleasant feeling when he is in church, and that he is unable to name any further moments. Such a conversation would perhaps proceed as follows:

J: Hmm, you know I've never really thought about that. It's just so strong in the church ... but hmm ... do I have it at other moments ...

P: Exactly, that's what I mean. Is that pleasantness something that is only connected to the church, or is it also connected to other moments?

J: I believe that it is only something that is connected to the church. It's also very pleasant when I go visit my grandmother, or when I recently had a good conversation with my father ... but that is a different kind of pleasantness than what I feel in church.

Of course, you have to honor what John says. John's answer here determines how you should proceed. You should not be disappointed that his pleasant experience is unique to the church. In fact, this answer offers new opportunities. Now you would focus on that difference he spoke about. What is that difference? Or, what makes the experiences connected to the church so unique?

Before going further, perhaps it's good to make a couple of cautionary remarks. First of all, the order of the various deepening interventions presented here really doesn't matter much. In other words, it's not as if you have to first ask the directee about feelings and images and then move on to concretising and broadening. Oftentimes it's better to simply choose the 'tool' that is most compatible with the directee, based on what he brings up, the impression you have of the person or, simply, your gut-feeling.

Secondly, note that in order to demonstrates the kinds of questions you could ask we have been exaggerating the example of Paul and John a bit. In 'real' accompaniment, it is advisable that you don't ask too many different kinds of questions during a single session. You must not make the directee feel uncomfortable, attacked, or under a sort of interrogation by approaching from too many angles. The example of Paul and John is provided as a pedagogical example more than a literal one.

Deepening Interventions 5: Exploring Fruits

Another deepening intervention that is focused on reality is about fruits. It asks the directee to identify where – in the world or in his life – glimmers of 'the Kingdom of God' have become already visible. This intervention is also grounded in the principle that there is more to spiritual accompaniment than merely interiority, or rather, that interiority has material expressions.

Take, for example, the novice whom we met earlier in this chapter. He suffered from dryness in his prayer, even as he encountered God during his evening walks in the garden. As he related his experience, he made use of the image of sitting on a bench together with God, and his novice master eagerly capitalised on that. The conversation proceeded well and they quickly found themselves discussing the novice's experience of having encountered God in the garden. I repeat here the final two sentences from that example:

> NM: And as you're sitting there with him, how does that go? Do you converse? Are you looking at each other?
>
> N: (*smiles*) You want to know what we do? It's as if he leans up against me a bit and I against him. Just like you would do with a good friend: shoulder to shoulder.

The novice master could proceed from here in a variety of ways. He certainly could zoom in on the inner elements that were mentioned. The intimate bodily experience of sitting 'shoulder to shoulder' would also be promising to delve into further. Another option would be to refer to how the novice was mourning his dry prayer life. What does the monastic tradition say about that, and does he find that helpful? The novice master could also connect the end and the beginning of the conversation. Now that he has reconnected to God's closeness, how does the novice look back on his earlier desolation? It could, perhaps, mark a new beginning in his relating with God in a different way; searching God in ordinary moments, not only in moments of explicit prayer or worship. It could even be possible that he begins to see God in a more this-worldly way, 'finding God in all things', so to speak.

However, sometimes it can be just as good to chart a new course and not to remain solely focused on internal things. As we have seen above, the director can ask the directee about the concrete details of an experience (this I called 'concretising') or ask whether this experience occurs more frequently and, if so, where and when ('broadening'). He can also ask the directee to talk about the fruits of the experience. That is what I would to discuss now. Let's take a look at how the novice master could approach the subject of fruits:

NM: What a special experience. You really are privileged that you experience God's closeness in such a way.

N: Yeah, now that you say it ... you're right.

NM: Could I ask you something regarding your experience that might come across as a strange question? I'm wondering what the fruit of this experience is for you. How do you go forth from such an experience? Does it impact how you respond throughout the day? Do you take something from that experience of God's closeness with you?

N: So, you're asking what I do with my experience afterwards? Or whether or not I feel like a better person? I do my best. Sometimes I succeed, other times not.

NM: No, sorry, that's actually not what I mean. I probably didn't explain myself very clearly. No, I'm interested in what you notice or find about yourself afterwards. This is not a question concerning your will power to become a better person, but, rather, of what simply is there, what you observe to be the case. To give an example, if I go for a run, afterwards I feel refreshed and can get to work with more energy. Or if I enjoy a glass of wine in good company, afterwards I notice that I am more attentive and patient. Do you ever notice something similar? Can you identify such a fruit?

N: Ah ok, yes, now I understand what you mean. (*pauses for a moment*) Well, I believe that afterwards I notice that I can better handle criticism. Normally I don't react well to criticism; you've seen that yourself. Since I started taking these evening walks, it's as if a space opened up within me that allows me to listen to people better. Sometimes I even feel that I can admit it when people are right, like, 'Yeah, I guess didn't wash the dishes well', or 'Maybe I was not very careful as a sacristan'. (*pauses for a moment, then smiles*) Yesterday Brother Mark pointed out that the chains on the thurible were all tangled in a giant knot again. I realised that I hadn't been very careful, and normally I would react and be defensive. But not this time. I smiled and started detangling the chains. (*moment of silence*) Could that be called a fruit of my experience?

NM: So, you've noticed a difference in how you deal with criticism, as if you have more space for handling it differently? Even if it relates to your own shortcomings, the things which you can't do so well?

N: Yes, space. At first the criticism here was threatening. If the brethren pointed out my faults, I felt so useless and so obsessive about trying to become someone different. Now, however, I have space to accept these things about myself. You're right, I guess. (*pauses for a moment*) It's not always like that, though. (*pauses again*) But sometimes, yes, it is. That's actually quite pleasant.

NM: That's pleasant, you said. And is that also a fruit?

N: Yeah, maybe? I'm not sure. What do you think?

NM: Well, you describe more it as something that happens than something you consciously do. Even more interesting is that you seem almost surprised, as if you had barely even noticed it. To me this seems indeed a fruit of the strong experience of God that continues to work in you.

N: Yeah, I think you describe it well. It's not as if I do this myself, as if I come up with a new supply of will power; it's as if it just happens to me. The only thing that I have to do is not to resist it, just give into it. (*pauses for a moment*) Just like my experience during my evening walks; that also just happens on its own.

The unexpected openness for criticism felt by the novice is a good example of what I mean by a fruit. The effect of God's touch is manifested concretely in that openness. This conversation is also a good example of the importance of this type of deepening intervention. If the novice master had not asked about fruits, then these experiences would have gone unnoticed by the novice. Only after he was asked about fruits does the novice come to the realisation that they are there, that something is different now.

By way of allusion to Ignatian jargon, I would call this a 'social consolation' (for more about consolation, see Chapter 2 and the Appendix). What I mean by this is that here consolation takes a primarily social form. God confirms the 'good' not just within me, but also through things happening around me and through my relationships with other people. Experienced spiritual directors will immediately recognise this form of consolation. For example, someone may typically report that his prayer life is dry while also noting that his partner notices that he is much calmer and more relaxed lately. Or someone on retreat reports that prayer isn't going very well, though she also notes that she is sleeping much better and that she feels peace in her body.

Careful, Courageous, and Reserved

Before concluding this chapter, I would like to make a few evaluative comments. Deepening questions are best handled with a wonderful combination of carefulness, courage, and reserve. The spiritual companion should not be too quick to intervene, but, rather, quite careful. At the same time, the companion has to take the lead in recognising new perspectives, and this requires that she does not shy away from inviting new perspectives. Yet the spiritual companion has to also remain detached, and so this calls for reserve. Let me elaborate these three words.

Because deepening questions have the potential to be intrusive and personal, one must always use them carefully. In a practical sense, they are only ever appropriate if there is something on the table which merits their use. You cannot just start asking such questions haphazardly. Recall that it was only after Esther talked a bit about what she meant with the energy she experienced that Renata was able to ask whether God had anything to do with it. Even if something is already on the table, so to speak, it's always better to begin with lighter interventions such as humming in recognition or mirroring. Recall that in the intimate and highly personal domain of spiritual direction, this is always the first thing to do. The lighter your intervention, the more friendly and inviting you are. If you move too quickly to the depths, the other will probably block you out.

We also saw this in the example of Esther and Renata; her first five interventions were all cases of mirroring (see Chapter 3) – and five is still quite a modest number! The advantage of first engaging in light and inviting interventions is that these interventions build rapport: they help you to get used to each other and to build trust. It's important that you have already been talking for some time before using deepening interventions.

Secondly, courage is also important – as long as it's expressed with moderation. In the deepening phase of direction, the director takes the leading role. By means of the deepening questions she posed, Renata played a major role in determining how the conversation proceeded.

Fourth Tool: Going Deeper

She took the initiative, as if she was saying 'we'll first try this, then that, and here is where we will delve into the depths'. This is the service a spiritual director typically provides.

At this stage, without your initiative, very little deepening would normally occur, unless the directee is 'self-directing' and that is exceptional. It is, therefore, necessary that you show courage and take the lead as the director. Thirdly, however, you have to use reserve. As Renata was taking the lead, a great deal of spiritual purity and simplicity was required. Her deepening questions must only aim at helping Esther. She must never pose a question out of curiosity – as a kind of 'spiritual voyeur' – and even less out of a feeling of superiority or sensation coming from her being the 'leader'. The only acceptable motivation is this: helping directees to talk about their spiritual life and God.

Closed Questions?

It may sound odd, but 'closed-ended questions' are an important aspect of deepening interventions; they in fact also pertain to the reserve we spoke of above. By means of closed-ended questions, the director gives the directee the opportunity to determine whether or not he wishes to continue with what you propose. While 'open-ended questions' are usually recommended for the type of conversation promoted in this book, they are not as open as their name suggests. For example, a director asking the open-ended question 'What does God have to do with X?' has already decided that God does indeed have something to do with the topic under consideration. (So much for the openness of the open-ended question.) In that way, an open-ended question forces the directee to speak about a topic that he has not had the opportunity to choose. When engaging in deepening conversation, it can therefore be very fitting to first pose a close-ended question, that the directee can answer with a 'yes' or a 'no'. In this way, the directee remains free to determine whether or not he wishes to embrace the approach that the director proposed. Renata's closed-ended question 'Do you think God has anything to do with this?' is therefore a very good beginning of the conversation with Esther on God.

Note that this observation regarding closed-ended questions also applies to the other interventions we've discussed in this chapter. For example, when asking deepening questions of the broadening type, it is better to begin by asking whether someone has had a particular experience in other circumstances. Then the directee is very free to admit whether or not this is the case. Conversely, if you begin by asking 'When did you experience this before?' you have already presumed that the directee will be able and willing to engage in broadening. When it comes to things such as images and representations, this strategy is also useful, because not everyone is a 'visual person'. An image can be a helpful entrance to deeper conversation for one person, but such language might make another person quite uncomfortable.

All the same, it is also true that the spiritual director doesn't have to always first start with a closed-ended question. As a director, you must always follow your intuition regarding what method is the best for the person sitting in front of you. Ask yourself: what is the most respectful way of proceeding here? What is the best way to bring about the sought-after deepening? What is called for here? Extra care? Directly driving the conversation forward? Showing a bit of reserve?

If the directee responds 'no' to your closed-ended question, nothing is lost. That might be painful for you to hear. You may be disappointed that your directee doesn't want to talk about God or that, according to him, God has nothing to do with the experience being discussed. Such instances require you to let go of your ego. These disappointments remind us once again of the need for spiritual asceticism: your own belief or spiritual insight that God has something to do with this situation is not being shared. You have to accept that your question, which you thought was right on the mark, was not. Still, nothing is really lost. Perhaps you posed the question at the wrong moment or perhaps you should have used a different wording. It might also be the case that your question was right on target but that the directee just needed a bit more time. In such a case your question has, at least, served to gently prod the directee. By means of your deepening question – whether of the broadening type, an image, or explicitly God – you have invited your directee to venture in new territory. Does it thereby already trace a pathway – even if the moment is not yet ripe for it to be fully explored?

Hiding

Finally, I'd like to make a few remarks about the directee's potential propensity to hide from or to avoid certain topics. At the moment that a spiritual conversation takes a deepening turn, from time to time your directee may noticeably try to avoid deepening. It's actually quite odd: at the very same moment we remove our shoes because we are standing on holy ground, we might become fearful, uncertain, or tempted to pull back. The closer God comes, the more inclined we are to run away. For example, when Renata asked Esther whether God has anything to do with her experience, she shied away from this topic. She had previously made use of the word 'grace', but she seemed to have forgotten that: 'Well, I think so. But I'm not totally sure'. In fact, she seemed hesitant to link this with God or Jesus: 'It's not as if I see a Jesus-figure in a white robe, speaking to me'.

This strongly resembles to how I already described 'hiding' in Chapter 4. In the literature, you often find this word coupled with a term borrowed from psychology, namely, 'resistance'. Resistance is not merely a factor in the course of spiritual accompaniment, but indeed in the whole of the directee's (and director's) life. For example, one's original dedication to prayer may be overgrown by the intensity of the 'daily grind'. The attention one is called to give to one's children, students, patients, or parishioners serves to dampen the original fire. Perhaps the busyness of life may even lead one to cynically doubt the original experience of God's closeness. In such circumstances it is correct to speak of a hiding from or avoidance of God; as God draws closer and closer to us, we hastily flee from him. This constitutes a 'resistance' to the intimacy God offers.

This temptation to hide can have many causes: the common human preference for what is known, the fear of change, the 'culture' of a particular church, society, or family, one's personal history or character traits, one's image of God, etc. It can also be a component of a larger spiritual dynamic wherein the Evil One discourages us in our growing relationship with God.

In such a case it is, above all, important to know how you as a director should react. The first step is to recognise the spiritual dynamic. You don't have to 'do' something immediately; it is sufficient to simply note that your directee seems to be trying to hide. A few signs of this hiding or resistance could be that you sense that reasoning starts to dominate the conversation in such a way that you move from the heart to the head, or you notice that the conversation has become slow and awkward, or you notice that the conversation is remaining on a very superficial level.

The second step is to bring the conversation back on track. That requires delicacy and wisdom as well as determination and resolve. Sometimes, as with Esther, this is best done as soon as possible. Sometimes, however, it's better to give people some time to wander in their thoughts – sometimes for five minutes, other times even up to a few sessions. When the time is right, how do you turn the conversation around? The simplest way is to bring up more spiritual topics or approaches, for which you will probably need the resolve that I just mentioned. However, sometimes it can be best or even necessary to explicitly thematise what's happening, perhaps even by means of a full explanation (for more on this possibility, see Chapter 8).

Margaret: A Widow Who Has Lost Her Faith in God

Margaret (sixty years old) is a long-time member of Pastor Anne's congregation in Chicago. Six months ago, Margaret lost her husband Peter to cancer. It happened very quickly: only three months elapsed between the diagnosis and his passing away. While Margaret was thankful that they had been able to say goodbye to each other and that she received many expressions of support and sympathy from her friends and family, she nonetheless felt shattered; the entire experience was extremely difficult and painful.

After the funeral, Anne and Margaret met regularly. Their conversations addressed various topics: that life felt so empty without Peter, that Margaret's children and others had been highly supportive of her, but also that she frequently felt so sad that she couldn't do anything at all. She also related how sometimes she would spontaneously burst into tears. Moreover, she expressed that she was grateful that Anne had been able to come and bless Peter before he died. Sometimes, she was able to convince herself to start cleaning the house and collecting Peter's clothes in an effort to move on. Finally, she shared that God felt far away from her and that she sometimes didn't go to church; she just couldn't get herself to go.

Usually, these conversations were marked by many tears. Anne tried to give Margaret all the room she needed. She understood her ministry to Margaret primarily as receiving her story without focusing in on one thing or the other and deliberately avoided the pitfall of offering pious platitudes. Nevertheless, even amid all the tears, there was evidence of some equilibrium; Margaret's own words suggested as much. Indeed, while talking about her intense sadness, she would eventually also mention how sweet and supportive her children had been throughout this difficult time, or how her neighbour would periodically stop by with some food or dessert. Clearly, Anne's receptive mode of listening had already borne fruit: she felt accepted in her sadness and this enabled her to notice some positive experiences as well.

In today's conversation, Margaret emphasises again that belief in God has become difficult and that it feels as if God is far away. These troubles

7: FIFTH TOOL

EVALUATING

The critical reader will have noticed that the terms 'God' and 'discernment of spirits' were conspicuously absent in the previous chapter's list with possible interventions for going deeper. These topics are indeed essential for spiritual accompaniment. They are tools that can be used not only to deepen the conversation – this was the focus of Chapter 6 – but also to evaluate what is being discussed. It is for this very reason that it seems important to treat God and discernment of spirits separately in this chapter, in which we explore the tool of evaluating.

Talking about God or discernment of spirits matters, because these conversations help us to discern the spiritual value of what is being said. Does the positive experience of a conversation you had wherein you vented to a friend indicate that this conversation was a good thing? Or, rather, is this positive feeling deceptive insofar as your venting took the form of gossiping about someone? Does your reticence to go out for a run this Sunday (you have a cold and are tired) point to an experience of responsible decision making or mere laziness?

I'll first demonstrate how this tool of evaluating functions by discussing the case of Margaret, in which discernment plays an important role. After this, we'll look at the topic of God. Finally, I'll explain that during spiritual accompaniment, the director should always keep God and discernment in mind.

Fifth Tool: Evaluating

have affected her Sunday morning routine; she avoids going to church. Up until now Anne has held herself back and not taken initiative in the conversation, mindful of the motto to take it easy in all things (see Chapter 3). Yet she has already met with Margaret a few times, whose sorrow has become less raw. Now that she brings up her struggle with God again, Anne decides to venture further down this path. Is now the time to explore this in some detail? Below is the dialogue between Margaret and Pastor Anne:

> M: It worries me lately that I find believing so difficult. God is so far away. Praying has become hard to do. I just can't get myself to go to church anymore; I've started regularly skipping Sundays. (*pauses*) Well, I know this is not the first time that I've told you this.
>
> A: Yeah, I'm so sorry, Anne.
>
> M: Yes, I am sorry too. (*pauses*) And ashamed. I think it is very bad.
>
> A: Ashamed and bad.
>
> M: Yes, ashamed and bad. (*pauses*)
>
> A: Can we take a closer look at this? Why don't we look a bit at that God who has become distant, at your feelings of shame, at your conviction that it's bad?
>
> M: What do you mean?
>
> A: Well, I'd be interested to know a bit more about all these things. But why don't we start with the first thing. You said that God is very distant. What is that experience like?

Up until now, this dialogue is an example of attentive and non-judgmental mirroring. Anne's agenda is to listen for what is alive in Margaret's soul rather than winning her over to resume her church attendance. Therefore, she shies away from questions like 'What would help you to start going to church again?' or 'What holds you back?' It's much too early to be that practical. Instead, she opts for looking more closely at what Margaret has shared and thereby opens the door to the core of spiritual accompaniment – deepening. For asking 'Can we take a closer look at this', she invites Margaret to articulate more precisely what is happening in her soul.

Moreover, the fact that Margaret herself stated that 'I know this is not the first time that I've told you this' suggests that her feeling of distance from God is vitally important to her. Anne could have chosen to mirror that sentence back to Margaret, for example, by repeating 'not for the first time'; that too could have worked as an invitation to say a bit more about that feeling. In this case, however, it seems that Anne has listened to Margaret for long enough to be comfortable with addressing the theme directly. The conversation proceeds as follows:

> A: So, what kind of experience is it, when God is so far away?
> M: It's like a dark room. The windows and curtains are shut. I don't see even a glimmer of light. There's no sound or music.
> A: Hmm.
> M: It's also cold. Very cold.
> A: It's dark, there's no sound, and it's cold.
> M: Yes. Actually, I'm starting to feel a bit cold right here as I say that.
> A: Hmm. Where do you feel that? Where do you feel the coldness?
> M: Pff, everywhere, actually. I usually start to shiver a bit. I'd like to go back to my bed with my winter duvet and an extra blanket. I hope that helps to get warm again.
> A: So you hope that you'll get warm again. What would it be like if you would feel warm again?
> M: Oh, then I'd get up! Rise and shine! That's how I would start the day: rise and shine! Let's get some things done today! But with that coldness and darkness, I think to myself: it's better to stay put; let's stay inside today.

Fifth Tool: Evaluating

A: Like you're protecting yourself from the stormy weather outside.
M: Yes, I withdraw. I hide. (*pauses*) But honestly, it not really nice inside.
A: No, I can imagine that it's not. You told me that it's cold, there's no music, no light…
M: Yeah, exactly. I don't like it.
A: And God isn't there either…
M: No, God isn't there either. (pauses)
A: (*smiles*) It sounds a bit like that story about Elijah where God wasn't found in the storm; neither was he in the darkness nor in the cold.
M: No. (*brief pause*) But where then? Where is God?
A: (*smiles*) Ha, yeah; if only we knew that!

Note how the deepening question 'what kind of an experience is that?' works. Margaret brings all sorts of images into the conversation. Also note that, while she does, Anne simply follows Margaret. The various images connect a bit, but not perfectly. That's not a big deal. You listen and follow. You could also have chosen to do so more subtly, for example by mirroring 'You feel a bit cold now' instead of asking the question 'Where do you feel that?'

At a certain point, Anne brings God back into the conversation: 'And God isn't there either?' As Margaret had mentioned God in the beginning of the conversation, you could consider Anne's intervention to be mirroring, for she responds to what the directee herself brought into the conversation. Anne's freedom in the follow up, namely by introducing Elijah, illustrates that spiritual accompaniment is not an impersonal technique. There is a chance that her association is off the mark, but that is no problem. On the condition that the rapport between the director and the directee is good, an 'incorrect' intervention will usually serve as a prompt for the directee to correct the director and say what she actually feels or thinks.

How does Anne best proceed with the case of Margaret? With heavy and 'negative' stories, the challenge for the director is always to give enough attention to them without overly dwelling on them. While doing this, the director should simultaneously be on the lookout for any glimmers of light. From a faith perspective, such glimmers are always there. What does that mean concretely; what should Anne do?

In the first place, she should respect Margaret by giving her space to express herself. Indeed, she has done so earlier, and she did so today. Usually directees come up with a variety of experiences; Margaret is no exception to this. In the second place, while listening, the director must be attentive for glimmers of light or hope. To say it boldly, the spiritual director's task is not to introduce light or hope, but to help the directee discover the light and hope that are already present. Margaret's story featured many traces of light and hope, such as her apparent desire for God's nearness. Anne could try something like, 'So God is absent; do I hear you saying that, somehow, you would want God to be more present?' This formulation, or something like this, doesn't come across as intrusive or forced; it's rather what has surfaced in Margaret's story itself. Again, you could consider it as a form of mirroring. Another possibility lies in the image of inside where it's dark and cold; the director could ask her about what has not yet been mentioned: outside. It is this option that I explore below.

> A: Could I try something? So, you're sitting inside, and it's not so pleasant; God is not there either. What is it like outside? Imagine that you go outside. How would that be?
>
> M: Ugh, outside. You know, I am not sure I even dare to think about that.
>
> A: Is it scary outside? Is that what you mean?
>
> M: Uhm… yes. Yes. (*pauses*) That's crazy, isn't it?
>
> A: Hmm.
>
> M: It is, right? It's not pleasant inside, and when you suggest that we take a look outside, I hesitate.

Fifth Tool: Evaluating

A: Hmm. And what if we went ahead and do it anyway? If we do it together?

M: Together?

A: Yes, so I'd go first, and you'd follow behind me. (*pauses*) Let's first open the door just a tiny crack. Can you see the tiny crack?

M: You're making a joke out of this!

A: (*smiles*) Yes, but it's a serious joke! (*more seriously*) What do you see as you look through the crack?

M: Hmm. Well ... I see the sun. I see a garden with flowers and the sun.

A: (*keeps silent*)

M: And I can hear children yelling. It's like a school playground during recess. Excited, joyful shouting.

Notice how useful your experiment of trying out something has become, for Margaret has started talking about a whole new dimension. Also note that the conversation is far from finished. Anne could easily deepen this, for instance, by asking Margaret to describe the flowers, to feel the sun, and so forth. In a later moment, after a bit of time – but not too quickly – she could (and should) return to God. For example, Anne may say: 'And God? God doesn't dwell in the cold or the darkness. And is God here: in the garden, the sun, the sound of joyful children?' Let's assume that Margaret answers positively to this question, agreeing that God is indeed here; he is present in the friendly invitation not to remain dead but rather to open herself to the sun, to flowers, to children's voices. Imagine that at the end of the conversation Anne asked about her husband. Possibly Margaret would share that she feels that he is quite close to her in these thoughts. That would be the moment to take up the evaluative tool of the discernment of spirits, which is the topic of the next section.

The Discernment of Spirits

Essentially, what discernment does is to attribute value to the various experiences that you have first carefully identified and then deepened. Its underlying assumption is simply that there are two types of experiences and that, in order to make good choices, it is crucially important to perceive the fundamental difference between these two types of experiences.

The first kind of experience has a feel of God, holiness, happiness, service, the Kingdom of God, tenderness, and so forth. In addition, it also leads to what it feels like, namely to God, holiness, happiness, service, the Kingdom, tenderness. While you could classify these experiences as good, note that we're speaking here of a spiritual and not a moral goodness. The second kind of experience is the opposite of the first. It has a feel of darkness, confusion, cynicism, egoism, not-God, rationalisations, cold logic, and so forth, and that is also what it leads to.

In saying this, the difference between the two kinds of experiences is immediately clear, for while God is part of the former, he is not of the latter. Hence the relevance of discernment. The stakes are high. What inspirations are we following? Whose voices are we heeding? In what direction are we going, towards God or evil?

However, you don't have to explain the entire theory of the discernment of spirits before you can use this tool. Moreover, you definitely don't have to use jargon like 'the good spirit', 'the bad spirit', and 'the angel of light'. To begin, all you have to do is to thematise the difference between the experiences themselves and then to explore what that difference means. Anne does this as follows.

> A: You know what strikes me, Margaret? It seems as if we've ended up in a whole different world.
> M: Yeah, I think so too …
> A: How would you describe the difference?
> M: Well, it's light now and it was dark. It was dead quiet, and now I can hear the sound of playing children.

A: Hmm.

M: And while God felt far away, absent really, in this new world he seems much less distant.

A: So, in the one world God isn't there, while in the other he is. And in the one world it's dead and quiet, while in the other there is life.

M: Yes.

A: I can't help but think of that saying of Moses: 'I hold before you life and death; choose life'. I think it's in the book of Deuteronomy.

M: Yeah, they are portrayed as standing in opposition to each other. (*pauses*) That's the case here as well.

A: And is Moses also saying something to you?

M: (*moved*) I think so ... the choice for life ... that's the choice for outside. For light. For God's friendly invitation to get up. Rise and shine!

A: You would choose life? Rise and shine?

M: Yes, I think that's what I have to do, to choose life. To deliberately choose that.

This dialogue illustrates how discernment works. Anne thematises the difference that she has noticed in the course of the conversation and invites the directee to join her in making an evaluation. The difference is not a neutral one: it has a meaning. Anne suggests what it could mean by alluding to the Bible text about life and death; here she takes a risk (cf. what I said earlier in this chapter about the director not needing to be impersonal). After Margaret's response indicates that this was both appropriate and helpful, Anne presses on and asks what Moses would have to say to her. This brings a breakthrough: Anne notices that she too is invited to choose life.

(Obviously, this is just one case. In other cases, you will have to look for other possibilities. Instead of suggesting an interpretation, as Anne does, you could also straightforwardly ask your directee what she thinks.)

Discernment really is a unique tool. Anne's intervention 'you know what strikes me', which was in fact simple mirroring, started a process that resulted in Margaret having a deeper insight into her experiences. In this sense, what Anne did qualifies as deepening too. Yet she didn't leave it at that but continued to look for meaning, distinguishing together with Margaret between what is worth pursuing and what isn't.

It's important to note again that discernment is infinitely more subtle than the question of whether or not something is positive or negative. It's not as if hope, light and life are always good and darkness and death are not, etc. For example, it's possible that the conversation would unfold as follows: first, Margaret is very angry at God, expressing this with deep sadness ('Why has God done this to me?'). Anne's listening, without correcting her or attempting to 'save' her, softens Margaret; her words become more relaxed. Is something like acceptance beginning to emerge here? Possibly an acceptance of her powerlessness in the face of her overwhelming sadness? In that case too, Anne can thematise that there is a difference. Now it is not about darkness and light, but about two kinds of sadness.

Last but not least, it is often very helpful that you at some point inform your directee what you're actually doing in this step. I will discuss this topic in the following chapter under the heading of formation. In that chapter, I will also discuss the related topic of actually making a choice and following through with it. Before we go there, in what remains of this chapter I would like to talk about a few other aspects of discernment, such as the question of God.

God

Interventions in which God is mentioned also qualify as tools both for deepening and evaluation. The example of Esther and Renata we looked at in Chapter 3 and 6 can here serve as an example too. Esther told her spiritual director that she has a great deal of energy and explained this by means of the image of a friend who unexpectedly but pleasantly comes by for a visit. I here repeat a piece out of that dialogue in order to show how God can be a 'tool' in spiritual accompaniment.

Fifth Tool: Evaluating

R: So when you say that your energy is a gift, a grace, that it's like someone who comes to visit, and things are well.

E: Yes, after such a meeting I feel very energetic again, very rich. (*smiles*) Then I can take on the world again!

R: (*with a smile*) And from what I'm hearing, that's exactly what you do, take on the world! (*pauses*) Does God have something to do with that energy, with that experience?

E: Well, I think so. But I'm not totally sure. It's not as if I see a Jesus-figure in a white robe, speaking to me.

R: So there's no Jesus-figure?

E: No.

R: And no God either, really?

E: Well, maybe God. I feel that the energy I receive is caring and loving. I can do a lot of good with it. I think I see something of God in that.

Even though there was ample occasion from the beginning of the conversation to address a religious perspective, Renata still took her time with it. After all, in the beginning of this example (in a part that was not repeated here) Esther herself introduced the word 'grace'. The advantages of taking it easy are manifest. Because the women are already in conversation for a while, the mutual trust between them has grown. A variety of material has been shared. Renata's patience has given Esther space for coming up with the example of drinking tea in the garden with a friend. Because of this, her question about God has a better chance of success than would have earlier been the case: there is something to talk about now.

Note that Renata begins with a closed question: 'Does God have something to do with that energy, with that experience?' By means of this, she gives Esther the choice to talk about God or not. It also serves as a kind of warning light for Esther: pay attention! Here's a new and vulnerable subject!

Also note that as Esther speaks about her struggles, Renata follows her in great freedom. If Esther is leaning more toward *No* than *Yes*, Renata calmly goes right along with her. She mirrors: 'So there's no Jesus-figure?' and 'And no God either, really?' This simple act of mirroring is precisely what brings Esther to say 'maybe'. There is great power in simple mirroring, with great flexibility, without fear of where it may lead, and without fear of being provocative. As we have seen in Chapter 4, attentive listening yields great fruit.

Still, in some cases, some insistence on the part of the director can be helpful. Imagine if Esther replied negatively that 'No, God doesn't have anything to do with this'. In that case, you could calmly express your surprise, reminding Esther of her earlier use of the word grace, which made you think of God. In this way, you take her negative answer seriously along with what she had previously mentioned. By doing this, a space is opened up where Esther can inform you what she meant by the word grace. If in Esther's mind grace is not associated with God, you can find out what she does associate grace with. Or perhaps you will discover that she is not accustomed to speaking about God.

Finally, your job isn't finished when the directee uses the word 'God'. At this point, it is important to invite the person you're accompanying to describe in greater detail what he means to say. What God is the directee experiencing or interacting with? And how do they interact? In Esther's case, there are many ways to do so. Perhaps the conversation could proceed as follows:

R: Alright. So God, just not a robed Jesus-figure.
E: Yeah, I've always found Jesus to be a complicated figure. He's so often presented as a super-human. You know, a muscular man in blinding white clothing... that really doesn't do anything for me.
R: And what about God?
E: God, yeah... (*pauses briefly*) When I think of God I immediately think of something in the very depths of my soul. I feel as if there is a love which has been implanted

Fifth Tool: Evaluating

> there. It's a bit like a source which is always bubbling up with water. Have you ever seen a real source, like a spring? Water just comes out of the ground and nobody knows where it comes from. I mean of course we can scientifically explain it, but you know what I mean.
> R: Yeah, I get it: it bubbles up, and that's what you experience within yourself.
> E: Yes, like a surprise.
> R: A surprise... what kind of surprise? A happy surprise?
> E: No, a bit like: what have I done to deserve this? How have I earned this?
> R: A bit like that friend who just happens to stop by for a visit?
> E: Yeah, a bit like that. But the difference now is that this is something going on inside of me. There's a source within me. The meeting with my friend is also a source but one which is outside of me. This source is in the silence and depth of my innermost self.
> R: And that has something to do with God.
> E: Oh absolutely. Maybe that's not what you think or what the Church thinks, but for me that's God. When I live from out of that source, I end up in a higher dimension. I have more strength and more love. That's what God means to me: to be powerfully loving.
> R: So not a Jesus dressed up in robes, but to be powerfully loving ... I'd say that sounds almost like a profession of faith.

Notice in this short dialogue how the director both calmly follows the directee and sticks to the theme at hand. Renata welcomes Esther's images and mirrors them back to her. She alternates between doing that on a small scale, when she pursues the image of the surprise, and on a large scale, when she recalls Esther's earlier use of the friend image. Because Renata follows Esther, she doesn't become confused or flustered when Esther seems to move away from talking about God and instead starts talking about a source. Yet after some time Renata mentions the word 'God' again. Note also that she doesn't succumb to the temptation of theologising over the Christian faith or Jesus the super-man. Instead, she focuses on Esther's inner movements. Something else to notice is the carefulness in her suggestion that the depth Esther brings up has something to do with God and seems a profession of faith.

God can be brought into the conversation in yet another way, namely, in the form of an invitation to turn toward God. In response to Ether's grace comparison, Renata could have also asked her if she had ever thanked God for it; after all, grace comes from God. If Esther would have said no, Renata could have invited her to try that – even here and now – and to then describe what happened. Afterwards, or if Esther had said yes, she could deepen that. How did the conversation with God go? What did she say to him? How did God react? What's it like to have a conversation with God?

The introduction of the term God can thus deepen the conversation in various ways. In this chapter, our focus is to demonstrate how, in addition, it also functions as a tool for evaluation. Out of Esther's previously unthematised and unexamined experiences of busyness, an image of God has emerged. This was first explained negatively (no robed Jesus-figure) before something positive emerged (a powerful love which helps her to live). An 'ordinary story' about a busy mum has turned into a deeply spiritual story about God. While Renata could certainly share this with Esther, even using these very words, she could also do so in a softer or more circumspect way, depending on what works best for Esther. Meanwhile she sees how Esther responds. Does she go along with what you're suggesting; does she agree? All of this is integral to discernment.

The outcome of the discernment has been that Esther's busyness appears to be a good thing, for Esther is able to find God in the midst of it, not as a robed Jesus-figure, but as the source of power and love. Sometimes busyness has an uneasy restlessness about it, which can be a sign of the evil spirit, but not so here. As I just said, another possible approach would have been for Renata to invite Esther to enter into a dialogue with God. That is a similar tool for evaluation, that would probably lead to a similar conclusion.

In this example, the word 'God' worked as a tool for evaluation. In other cases, you may need to be bolder and more direct. Imagine that you're talking with a church-going college student who still lives at home with his parents. He is deeply unhappy and is seriously considering giving up his studies and moving away from home. He deeply longs to go out and see the world. Once you have listened receptively to him – and *only* then – it might be useful to ask him quite bluntly something like: 'and what do you think God would have to say about your plan?' There is a fair chance that a faith perspective may bring him some good insights. Perhaps this triggers confirmation of his plan at a deeper layer. Conversely, maybe this question prompts him to abandon a potentially crazy plan; your question functioned like a cold shower that woke him up from his delusion. There is also a chance that your question serves as a confronting mirror: perhaps God is inviting him to take a good look at what is really causing his unhappiness. What is he running away from? What is he hoping for? The bottom line is that you never know what your question stirs up. You only know that it may well help to explore the spiritual-religious meaning of the student's experience of unhappiness. If it works, it turns the conversation into a process of evaluation and discernment.

The Atmosphere

Up until now, I've presented evaluation as being a specific moment in the conversation. After attentively listening with a focus on inner movements and depth, you then evaluate the material that's out on the table. In fact, that is too schematic a presentation. A good spiritual companion has discernment always on her mind: she is constantly monitoring whether or not the conversation is proceeding in a good way. That too is a form of evaluating. What sorts of things should you pay attention to in this monitoring process? And what should you do?

The first thing you should pay attention to is the mood or atmosphere.

What do you notice in the directee, particularly during the conversation? You can easily notice obvious signs of cynicism, frustration, exuberance or tenderness. The fact is, however, that a person who feels agitated can come across as quite calm. Or the conversation might feel superficial, while it actually points to feelings of peace and stillness. Sometimes you don't know, and you should take note of that too. Don't let yourself be fooled by pious or spiritual words. Someone may say much about God and faith, but in a way that is hard, or maybe even harsh. At the same time, someone may not speak directly about God, but emit a peaceful simplicity that indicates that God is, indeed, present. In short, what you want to notice is the atmosphere conveyed by what the directee says, not necessarily the words that he uses.

In identifying the mood or atmosphere, you should be mindful of the two types of spiritual experiences which I delineated earlier in this chapter. Is it an atmosphere that is open to God, in which you hear something of holiness, happiness, service, the Reign of God, gentleness, and so forth? Or do you sense angst, confusion, unhappiness, gloominess, or egoism?

If you suspect the former, then your 'only' task is to remain there and stay with that experience, and possibly thematise it a bit. For example, if Margaret talks about her sadness in a way which suggests healthy acceptance of it, that is a strong indication that you're on the right track. In that situation, you could invite her to share a bit more and then evaluate it together along the lines I've sketched earlier. You could also thematise the mood of the conversation; by doing so, the conversation itself becomes the starting point, an occasion for spiritual deepening.

You do have to change course, however, if you notice that the mood is of the second sort. In this case, you have more work to do. You should first try to figure out what is the cause of the mood. Is the conversation addressing something that, while unpleasant, is actually going in the right direction? Or, conversely, does the negative mood have no positive meaning at all? What can you do in the latter scenario? The tools provided in this book work also for approaching negative, unhelpful atmospheres: listening, following, exploring, and while doing so, trying to pay attention to the atmosphere of the conversation. If it does not become or remain good, then you're probably on the wrong track; it's your job to determine where you suspect the light might be. For example: if you notice on further exploration that Margaret's experience of God's absence is not leading to light – as we in fact saw – then you should find a way to change course. If you don't do this, you risk becoming imprisoned in a world that has nothing to do with God, salvation, wellbeing, or the Kingdom. Yet conversely a conversation which addresses busyness can turn out to be a very spiritual one, as was the case with Esther.

It's impossible to know beforehand what kind of experience you're dealing with. For this reason, attentive listening is so important. The English say that the proof of the pudding is in the eating. By more closely considering a particular experience, you will be able to notice how the mood develops. For example, acceptance can turn out to be pseudo-acceptance: forced, superficial, and fearful. In such a case, rationalisation can serve as a smokescreen that looks like acceptance. In the case of Esther, it turned out that the mood of busyness actually had a profoundly spiritual depth. In all cases, this is the way you have to test the waters: you suspect something, you follow, you see how things develop, then you come to a conclusion.

The Fruits: The Kingdom of God

Besides this, it is also very useful to pay attention to something else: the fruits. Is the Kingdom of God springing up in the directee's life? Are compassion, goodness, gentleness, simplicity, and clarity emerging? Or is the opposite happening?

When I was in secondary school, I would sometimes go visit my grandfather on Saturday afternoons. 'Today it's your turn', my mother would tell me, and she would point to a thermos filled with coffee already prepared for me on the kitchen counter. Even though I rarely felt like visiting, afterwards I noticed that my grandfather was very happy that I had come over. In fact, it was really good just to be able to sit with him for a bit. I would say something, and this would be followed by a period of awkward silence. I can still picture his large and rough hands; he had been a farmer. Even though those visits were a bit awkward, it was still a good thing to be with him. 'Bye, Jos, tell your mother I said hello and be sure to thank her for the coffee'. 'Bye grandpa'. In these sorts of cases, it's the external things rather than the inner movements or feelings which indicate that we're doing the right thing. That is what I mean with the fruits.

Imagine that your directee is a man in his forties with a rather complex job. Your conversation together mostly addresses his dilemmas: 'Should I confront my boss? Should I just quit? Does God really want me here? What other kind of job would I like to have?' But in the midst of all of this, he also says something about his colleagues. Now and again they come to his desk to have a chat; just the other day, one of his younger colleagues said that she really appreciated his calm and wise presence. Ah, there's a small glimmer of the Kingdom. He continued by recalling that his boss also recently came to ask his advice about a complicated file, and that they were together able to make sense of it. Well, there you go – another sign of the Kingdom.

This notion of fruits is also relevant when talking about someone's prayer life. Take the example of a young student who lives in an ecumenical community and is trying to enrich her prayer life. Even though this is something very important to her, she is frustrated that it just doesn't appear to be working. As you're talking about this, she says a few things about her friends who are really happy with her. She almost drops that line by accident, but as you inquire a bit further, it turns out that her fellow community members also think that she's an ideal housemate. The superior of the house, in fact, just told her that she brings tremendous joy into the wider group. These sort of fruits of God's Kingdom suggest that she is solidly on the right track. Perhaps her struggles in prayer need to be seen in light of the overall picture, which is actually very positive.

How are you supposed to react to the fruits of the Kingdom? First of all, you have to have an eye ready and attentive to seeing them. This should be one of the things which you are constantly on the lookout for: do you see any fruits of the Kingdom? Subsequently, it's good to thematise these fruits. If you notice any, you should try to develop the conversation as in the example with Esther: simply invite the directee to explore these fruits more deeply and then move into spiritual evaluation.

What complicates the matter is that, in addition to fruits, another 'spirit' may be at work. For example, in the case of the student who was frustrated about her prayer life, the spirit of frustration probably has little or nothing to do with the Kingdom of God. In such an instance, the example of the recently widowed Margaret is a good model to follow for elaborating both 'spirits', after which you thematise the difference and continue the conversation from there.

It's important to indicate how significant this topic of fruits of the Kingdom really is. By remaining attentive to the Kingdom of God present around us, we avoid the pitfall of only being attentive to personal-individual interiority, as is the case in many forms of contemporary spirituality. We should also note that Ignatian spirituality risks falling into this trap. While earlier I made an appeal for 'affective orthodoxy' and the importance of developing a deeper sense of the inner life in the Church, I would now like to add that this has to be balanced. The key to this balance is maintaining a sense of 'externalised holiness' or what I would call in more Ignatian jargon 'social consolation' (also briefly treated in Chapter 6). Externalised holiness or social consolation forms a quintessential complement to affective-internal faith and spirituality.

Concluding Remarks

This chapter treated the evaluation of the directee's spiritual experiences and spiritual life. Not everything that glitters is gold, even when the directee speaks about God. Being able to assign a value to what is said is, then, of the upmost importance.

There is, of course, much more that can be said about discernment. Barry and Connolly indicate, for example, that good fruits never come alone. You can never have 'only' patience, or 'only' peace. If you have one good fruit, it usually goes together with such things as gentleness, simplicity, kindness, and so forth. Barry and Connolly also helpfully remind us not to focus too much on determining whether what a directee says about their faith is orthodox or not. The workings of the Spirit are, indeed, broader than these categories. At the same time, it does not bode well if a directee is so self-absorbed in his own subjective world that he does not accept any questions or alternative approaches.[60] Further, I could have added other important examples to the ones discussed in this chapter. However, as this book is no more than a basic guide to practice, perhaps two final comments will suffice.

The first is to say that it's not a problem if the spiritual director does not to know immediately what to think of the directee's story. Rather, one could even argue that this is a good sign. After all, it is the Creator who is interacting with the creature. That relationship is always a mysterious one and can never be fully grasped by you as the director. It's more appropriate to think of yourself as a witness to this relationship rather than as a detective. Even if you really do have an idea of what is going on, you must always maintain a radical openness. Therefore, you shouldn't become nervous when you're unsure. In such a case, all you have to do is engage in some discernment together. If you need to, you can even lay your cards out on the table: 'I see various options here and I'm uncertain which is the correct one'.

Secondly, the moment of evaluation is, in a certain way, also a 'check' of your earlier choices. If you do not get to the point of evaluation, then you may have dwelt a bit too long on the surface so that you have nothing deeper to evaluate. Maybe you didn't follow the directee attentively enough so that the directee didn't feel safe to open up further. Or, perhaps you didn't help the directee to focus on and deepen what was said. Such things can happen and are not necessarily a bad thing. You're only human, so there is always a chance that you are not as 'sharp' as you should be. These are learning opportunities! Moreover, the person that you accompany can also be quite adept at hiding herself (see Chapters 4 and 6), or she simply may be having a bad day. (By the way, well done for observing that it was not a perfect conversation!) If you regularly

---

60 For the indicated 'nuggets' and yet more besides, consult the very helpful chapter, 'Criteria for Evaluating the Religious Dimension of Experience' in Barry, Connolly, *The Practice of Spiritual Direction*, pp. 107–123.

Fifth Tool: Evaluating

seem unable to arrive at the point of discernment, you may need some supervision to analyse what is happening. While carefully anonymising the content, consider taking your imperfect session to someone with directing experience and consult with them about how the conversation unfolded. What could you do differently, as a spiritual director? What could the directee do differently?

8: SIXTH TOOL

FORMING FOR SPIRITUAL MATURITY

A final tool aims at the directee's growth in spiritual maturity. Rather than making the directee dependent on your own spiritual insights and practical wisdom, your job as a spiritual director is to enable him or her to gradually navigate his or her own unique course in spiritual life. As we saw in Chapter 2, this is one of the core values of Ignatian spiritual accompaniment; it relates to the direct, un-mediated contact between Creator and creature that the director is supposed to respect and foster. But how does forming for spiritual maturity work concretely? In this chapter, I will give a few examples. Note that the point of the chapter at hand is not to address the forming in particular domains of spiritual life, such as learning various forms of prayer or dealing with distractions in one's prayer life.

The Topics You Wish to Discuss (and Those You'd Rather Not)
A first type of formation consists in explaining just what kind of conversation it is that you're trying to have. What sorts of things are good topics for conversation, and which ones are less so? For example, it's best not to talk too much about theology, but what pertains to spirituality is perfectly appropriate. It's better to talk less about other people and more about oneself. Ultimately, spiritual direction focuses on experiences more than on information, facts, events, encounters, or beliefs.

Imagine that you're having a session with Tony, a man in his forties with a comfortable government job. He's recently returned from a business trip to Paris. After finishing his meetings, he had the opportunity to visit Sacré-Coeur. By the time he got there, it was already late, and the tourists had all gone home: the church was nothing an oasis of peace and quiet. As Tony sat down, he was overcome by a strong sense of being home, of feeling that this was the place where he was meant to be. The experience made a deep impression. It awoke, so he says, a long dormant desire to become a Catholic, and for this reason he contacted the parish office. The pastor placed him on the usual Rite of Christian Initiation for Adults (RCIA) trajectory together with other possible converts. But Tony is also very interested in further exploring the experience he had in Sacré-Coeur: namely, the feelings of peace and his resurrected desire to become a believer. For this reason, the pastor suggested that Tony meet with you – below indicated as the 'SD' (spiritual director) – for a bit of spiritual direction. After an initial 'getting to know you' conversation that also included some explanation on the nature of spiritual accompaniment, you now meet each other for the second time:

SD: Welcome, Tony! How is it going?
T: Quite well, thanks!
SD: I take it that the RCIA sessions have begun. Are you enjoying them?

The SD then proceed to have a short conversation about the RCIA sessions, the other participants, and so forth. The SD is warming up. After a short time, the SD directs the conversation to a further step.

SD: So if I remember correctly from our last conversation, you also wanted to talk a bit about your personal experiences. Is that right?
T: Yes, that's right. If we can?

SD: Absolutely! Where would you like to start?
T: Well, perhaps with my experience in Sacré-Coeur. I think it's a bit strange, actually. I'm in Paris on a business trip, and I suddenly pop into a church after a busy workday. I'm the kind of person who will only go into a church on Christmas and Easter, so even deciding to walk into the church was a bit weird. Not really like me. But I don't know, I just felt so comfortable there …
SD: Looking back on it, it's all just a bit weird.
T: Yes, weird. Almost as if it was meant to be; like I was sent there or something.

It's pretty clear where you should focus on in this conversation: the experience in Sacré-Coeur. But you're still not sure what exactly happened there. Tony's use of the words 'weird' and being 'sent' are in fact of little help. They invite a theological evaluation of what happened, but you don't want to go there yet. For now, you just want to stay with Tony's experience. One way to do that is by concretising (see Chapter 6).

SD: Weird, you say. Hmm. Tell me a little more about when you were in Paris.
T: What do you mean?
SD: Well, how was the city? How was your business trip? How about your walk up to Sacré-Coeur?
T: It was the springtime, a bit warmer than here. Paris is truly a beautiful city, but you probably know that already. I usually visit each year for work. Normally I would stay at a hotel in the business district of La Défense, but this time my secretary booked me into a hotel close to Montmartre. She said it was 'great deal' even if it was a tad longer of a Metro ride, but the difference was pretty

negligible. Maybe it was all just meant to be. (*pauses for a moment*) Do you believe that some things are meant to be? Is that something compatible with the Catholic faith?

SD: And what happened then? So you're staying in a hotel in the neighbourhood, but how did you end up in the church?

T: Oh, well, that was a bit of a coincidence. But what about things that are meant to be? Do you believe in that?

The conversation now sits on two separate tracks. Tony wants to talk about the meaning of things that are meant to be; you want to talk about his soul. You tried to ignore Tony's question, but that was not lost on him. If you don't do something, the conversation risks becoming a sort of wrestling match or tug-of-war: Tony wants to discuss this, you want to discuss that. You're not going to get out this space unless you tell him a little about the meaning of spiritual direction and what he should expect from your conversations. You may have done so during your intake conversation, yet the penny has clearly not dropped. You're going to have to explain that, aside from his rational questions, there is also the domain of spiritual experience. It is the latter that you're interested in, because you suspect that you're able to find God there. In short, you have to do a bit of formation. You could continue as follows:

SD: (*smiles*) I can't help but smile. You want to talk about thoughts and convictions: that something is *strange* or *meant to be*. I want instead to talk about what it is that you actually experienced, and what happened in your soul. You're into theology, whereas I'm into spirituality. I just want to know what it was you actually experienced sitting there in Sacré-Coeur.

T: (*interrupts him*) But haven't I said that already? I told you that it was weird and that the more I thought about it the more I wondered whether or not it was meant to be?

SD: Yes, but you know, I'm really interested to hear more. I suspect that you lived through a very rich experience there and that God was very close to you in that moment. That experience might be able to tell us quite a bit about who God wants to be for you or how God communicates with you. More than anything, it might be able to give you some real insight in these matters. That's what motivated my questions about your day, how you ended up in that church that night, and what happened.

T: Ah alright. I guess I can try. What do you want to know?

SD: Perhaps we can start by going through the various things you experienced during that afternoon and evening. Do you still remember what time you finished up with work? Did you have far to walk afterwards? Where did you choose to sit inside the church? Let's start with that; later we can zoom in on what you experienced.

By telling Tony about the kind of conversation you are striving to have here, you're engaging in formation. You allow Tony to have a look at your game-plan and then you invite him to join you. Note how modest the formation is in this case. Your main focus is on having a conversation about Tony's soul; you're not giving a mini-seminar about the objectives of spiritual direction.

It's quite conceivable that you do some more formation later on, perhaps in a more extensive form, if the conversation about Tony's experiences gives you good occasion. At that point you could, perhaps reflect back on how valuable it actually was to focus on Tony's soul. This is something you would have missed if you started talking about theology as Tony had suggested. At that point, perhaps you could even make larger connections and refer to the existence within the Church of a variety of spiritual traditions that promote interiority (something that Tony probably doesn't know much about). You always should exercise restraint. You're a spiritual director. When it comes to Tony's theological questions, suggest that he explore those in the RCIA sessions.

The same logic holds true in other cases, for example, if the conversation moves to talking about other people, or if too much is being said about what happens in the world or at home. In both cases, it takes some skill to move the conversation to addressing the directee's soul. Sometimes this requires explicit explanation to help the directee understand what spiritual accompaniment is about. That's what I mean by formation.

Why You Persist in Asking

You also engage in formation when you explain why you persist in asking questions. Asking questions is an important aspect of spiritual direction, related both to active listening and deepening. Sometimes this questioning seems awkward, or it may even provoke irritation. This too can be an occasion for some explanation and, therefore, formation.

Imagine that Tony follows your suggestion: the conversation begins to address what he experienced sitting in the church. He tells you that he had a normal day with nothing really out of the ordinary: negotiating, talking numbers, making deals. Normally everyone would go out for a drink after work, but he wanted to work on some emails back at the hotel. For one reason or another, he made a slight detour to Sacré-Coeur and seated himself at the back of the impressive basilica. And that's when 'it 'happened'. Your dialogue with him continues as follows:

SD: And then it happened …
T: Yep. Then it happened. (*smiles*) But I have difficulty describing what actually happened, and you probably want to know about that.
SD: (*smiles back*) You can see right through me! (*looks interested*) Can you try to describe it? You sat down, and what did you notice then?
T: I noticed that there was a lot of room and that everything was so quiet. That church is just so incredibly beautiful.

> Then, as I opened my eyes, I saw an immense mural of Jesus. He looked so inviting. I don't think he is beautiful, by the way, but his pose is certainly very inviting.

Tony is not exactly jumping into the deep end. This shouldn't really surprise in the light of his inclination to talk ideas rather than the soul. Nevertheless, he mentions a few things which are possible inroads towards a spiritual conversation. You could either choose one, or you could choose to keep the various options open and see what happens. In what follows, the spiritual director chooses the latter option: he lists the various elements of Tony's answer.

SD: So it started with noticing how large and quiet the space was, and then you noticed the mural of Jesus. You were also sitting there with your eyes closed for a time.

T: Yeah, I just felt so welcome. That depiction of Jesus with his open arms … It was almost as if he was looking directly at me. Well, I mean, not really of course. But it felt a bit like that. Or do you think that's strange?

SD: Ah, okay. You were sitting there and you had the feeling as if Jesus was looking right at you. (*pauses*) How did that feel?

T: Pff, actually, I don't know. It was really special. But beyond that, it's difficult for me to describe.

SD: And if you mentally transport yourself back to that moment? Do you still remember what appealed most to you? Was it Jesus' eyes? His hands? His voice? Or just the general atmosphere around him?

T: I think it was his posture. It made me feel at ease. Maybe that was the reason why I felt so welcomed.

SD: So Jesus' posture put you at ease and made you feel welcome.

T: Yes. You know, I've never really felt at home in the Church. I always think that I don't really belong there because I don't follow all of the Church's rules. And I get irritated at the hypocrisy. So I usually avoid churches, really. I don't belong there.

SD: Yes, I can imagine.

T: But then I found myself in a church. And instead of feeling guilty or irritated, I felt that I was welcome.

SD: And how would you describe that feeling of being welcome?

T: What do you mean?

SD: Would you say that it was like a warm breeze on a chilly day? An unexpected moment of happiness? A relief? Was it liberating? What did you feel?

T: You're not accepting my answers! Whatever I say, you always ask me more questions! Questions, questions, questions …

Tony is clearly not yet used to this, and he's having some trouble putting his experience into words. Nevertheless, the conversation is slowly but surely moving in the direction of a spiritual conversation. You haven't allowed yourself to become distracted by his asking 'Do you think that's strange?' and instead remained focused on following and listening deeply to him. The questions you asked played an important role. This is, however, delicate: maybe too many questions were posed. Possibly this made the directee feel powerless, exposed, or tongue-tied. Spiritual directors have to be careful. Sometimes it's better to give the directee a moment to catch his breath and refrain from asking any more questions – even when various possibilities for going deeper are clear. At the same time, however, posing questions is unavoidable, all the more so with people who are not yet acquainted with their own soul.

It's not necessarily a bad thing that Tony expresses his irritation with all of the questions you asked. Even if he didn't say it directly, you would probably be able to sense it. Whether it's said implicitly or explicitly, Tony's irritation at these questions is an occasion for formation. At this point you could explain why you're asking all of these questions. You're doing this not because you want to control the conversation, and not to make Tony jump through ever-higher hoops, and even less out of an inappropriate curiosity about Tony's private life. The goal is, simply, to help Tony become acquainted with God's manner of communicating with him. After all, it really seems as if God has granted Tony clear signs of his presence; it would be a shame to not notice them. The explanation might proceed as follows:

SD: I'm sorry, Tony. You're right: this really is a rapid-fire round of questioning. Just when you think that you've answered a question and are off the hook, then another question follows immediately! Sorry, that was not my intention.

T: No, but it is what you're doing! It feels like an interrogation!

SD: Hmm, yes. Do you mind if I say a little bit about why I'm asking all of these questions? Do you remember why we started meeting in the first place? As I recall it, you not only wanted catechetical instruction, but you also wanted to revisit the experience you had in Paris. That's right, isn't it?

T: Hmm.

SD: Well, that's what I'm trying to do: to reconsider that experience. But that's not so easy. Frequently, people recognise a special experience when they have one, but have a hard time describing what made it so special. All I'm trying to do is discover this together with you. What was this experience, actually? Perhaps you can see that all of my questions are trying to figure this out.

T: Yeah, I see what you mean. But these are all difficult questions, and that makes it annoying.

SD: I understand and I'm sorry about the annoyance. I'd compare this to learning a new language. The first thing you have to do is to learn to pronounce new letters. This made me crazy when I was learning Hebrew: so many different letters, so many different sounds ... you and I are also learning to speak a new language: the language of your soul. It's a very delicate language, because it's a language of feelings, affections, and of being touched deeply. Sometimes, the letters and words are very clear, as was the case with you in Paris; sometimes, however, they are light and subtle. Spiritual accompaniment has to do with talking about these things, discovering them together, and then seeing what God has to do with them.

This is formation: you explain what spiritual accompaniment is about. Even more important: you explain what one's inner and spiritual life is about. The goal of formation of this kind is the other person's spiritual maturity. Could you have offered up that explanation more quickly? Possibly. On the other hand, it is also advisable to take it easy, perhaps keeping things more anecdotal and lighter, as in the above example. In any case, spiritual accompaniment must not become a seminar, a catechetical class, or a lecture. The spiritual director should always keep in mind the ultimate focus, which is the directee's spiritual experience itself, and therefore return that. 'Now that it's clear why I asked you all of these questions, shall we get back to your experience?'

Examples and Exercises

You can also engage in formation by giving examples or small exercises. These are very concrete and practical kinds of formation. Imagine that you and Tony are, in fact, able to return to a consideration of his experiences. However, it's very difficult. Tony is just not able to find the right words. It's clear that asking more questions won't accomplish anything. Luckily, there are other means of moving toward the level of spiritual conversation, and these are also formative, such as giving examples. This would proceed as follows:

T: Yeah, I see what you mean by a new language. But I'm not familiar with this language, and so I find your questions annoying. I mean, I know that they're good questions … but I just can't answer them. I honestly don't even know where to begin looking for answers.

SD: Hmm. (*pauses*) Let me give you an example from my own life. My father died a few years ago. I ended up having to arrange many things myself because I'm the most churchy member of the family: writing the obituary, arranging the funeral, designing the prayer card. I didn't have much time to mourn. The fact that I had lost my father didn't really phase me then because I was so busy. I only really started mourning my father a few weeks later. It all hit me one day when I was sitting in a cafe in Dublin. I was looking out over the water from my table, and it all just hit me like a ton of bricks: my father is dead. It was very unique: I felt both grief and consolation. I was just sitting there all alone at my table. I began to sense the weight of my empty hands: alone, empty, without my father. I felt like a tree in winter without its leaves. And yet, I also felt something light, like a crocus popping up out of the cold, dark earth. It was a bit like a smile – not a smile from anyone in particular, but simply a smile. For me, this experience had a lot to do with God: both the sorrow of emptiness and the consolation of a smile (*remains silent*).

T: What a beautiful story.

SD: Thank you. I shared this story because I suspect that the vocabulary helps to articulate your experience in Paris. You're the only one who knows which words work best.

> But I suspect that it has something to do with being empty or full, saddened or comforted, smiling or weight, lightness or heaviness.
>
> T: Hmm. Yes. It doesn't have to do with sadness, but more with that smile you talked about. I felt as if God was right there and that he was very friendly. As if he said: 'It's really great that you're here', without any critical or moralising comments.
>
> SD: Alright. So God was friendly.
>
> T: Yes, he looked friendly. You know how it is when you can sense someone is friendly just by looking at their eyes? They don't have to say much, but you can just see it. That's how it was with God.

From this point, you can clearly continue to go deeper by asking questions: what was it like to be in the company of this friendly God? What kind of feeling did this give you? What changed at that point? (For options for deepening, see Chapter 6).

Another method of concrete and practical formation is to give your directee some exercises to do – a bit of homework, so to speak. For example, you could ask her to write down in a daily journal the feelings she experienced or the moments of her consolation or desolation. When it comes to assigning these exercises, it's best to mould them to each person's tastes and disposition. For example, if someone is a big music fan, perhaps you could ask her to consciously listen to a piece of music and then ask her to write down a few reflective thoughts on the experience. You could do similar things with regard to someone who loves nature, or someone who loves to be social with people. You can certainly also make it a bit more religiously tinted by inviting the person you accompany to write down things like: Did she feel God during the day? Was God close or far away? What was that like? And so on. Exercises like this foster an awareness of what goes on in the soul.

By way of conclusion of this point, I would like to make three brief comments. First of all, we have seen that Tony was pretty proficient in verbally letting you know that, while he understood what you were trying to do, he was having trouble with it. In other cases, the directee may be less verbal: indeed, feelings of helplessness and discomfort can also be expressed non-verbally. It does not matter if the directee is verbal or not: you can still respond in the same ways we've outlined here.

Secondly, in our example above the spiritual director provided an example from his own life. While that usually works well, the director could also provide examples from other sources: Scripture, the lives of the saints, friends, culture, current events, or even examples from other spiritual accompaniments (made completely anonymous, of course). Moreover, when it comes to the exercises you might assign, it's always a good idea to allow the directee to think *with you* in order to come up with something. What could she do in order to become more familiar with the world of the soul, with her experiences, feelings, and spirituality?

Thirdly, the example of Tony actually worked: all is well that ends well. However, you should be prepared that, sometimes, your efforts won't work. In such cases, assigning exercises is probably a good help, but sometimes even that won't work. You might have to be patient and wait for better times to come. It could also be, in such cases, that you're not the best fit as a spiritual director for someone, or that Ignatian spirituality is not a good fit for this individual.

Explaining What You're Hearing

Another important formational moment is explaining what you're hearing as the directee is speaking. By doing this, you're providing the directee with a frame of reference, words, and concepts which may help her determine what is happening in the soul. As this can only happen if you've been listening for a while, I'll use the example of Margaret who was struggling with her faith in God after the death of her husband (from Chapter 7).

In that case, we saw that Margaret was able to imaginatively describe how she felt without God: like being in a cold and dark house. Through the skill of her pastor, she was also able to imagine the outdoors and the

Sixth Tool: Forming for Spiritual Maturity

voices of children. I here again take up the dialogue from the point that Anne focused her attention on the difference between being inside and being outside.

> A: You know what strikes me, Margaret? It seems as if we've ended up in a whole different world.
> M: Yeah, I think so too …
> A: How would you describe the difference?
> M: Well, it's light now and it was dark. It was dead quiet, and now I can hear the sound of playing children.
> A: Hmm.
> M: And while God felt far away, absent really, in this new world He seems much less distant.
> A: So, in the one world God isn't there, while in the other He is. And in the one world it's dead and quiet, while in the other there is life.
> M: Yes.
> A: I can't help but think of that saying of Moses: 'I hold before you life and death; choose life'. I think it's in the book of Deuteronomy.
> M: Yeah, they are portrayed as standing in opposition to each other. (*pauses*). That's the case here as well.
> A: And is Moses also saying something to you?
> M: (*moved*) I think so … the choice for life … that's the choice for outside. For light. For God's friendly invitation to get up. Rise and shine!
> A: You would choose life? Rise and shine?
> M: Yes, I think that's what I have to do, to choose life. To deliberately choose that.

It's probable that Margaret found this conversation very special and that she was able to feel how special it was. But it's also possible that she's not yet able to fully explain what's happening. If Pastor Anne is able to assist her with that – by engaging in some formation – she would help Margaret see the unique and special beauty of what she has just said. This formation would highlight how God communicates with Margaret. The conversation might go something like this:

A: Margaret, I think what you've just shared with me is so beautiful and moving.

M: Thank you. Yes, I also think it's beautiful. It also makes me feel more relaxed. You did that so well.

A: That's nice of you to say. If you wouldn't mind, I'd like to share with you why I found it so beautifully moving.

M: Oh, well, now you've made me very curious!

A: (*laughs*) Alright, well let me try my best. I deeply believe that God wants only good things for us. Nevertheless, God can't prevent death or suffering. But God can accompany us through all of these moments. I know that you know this already, but I'd also say that this is vital spiritually. In any and everything that happens to you, God will support you: God will always give you courage, hope, trust, and perspective. These are things you can feel internally. But there is also another power at work that is not of God; let's call this evil. This power will try to do precisely the opposite of what God does. It will make things so unbearably heavy, sad, difficult, and cold. Margaret, as I listen to your story, it's almost as if I can hear these two powers at work within you. I mean, of course it's normal to feel intense sadness at the loss of your husband. It takes time to work through this, and it's normal that the sun doesn't shine again immediately. But the kind of heaviness you're experiencing, that you feel you've lost God, and that it's cold and dark – that sounds like the influence of evil. That new perspective you received, of wanting to go outside and hearing the children's voices: that is much lighter. Could that be God?

M: *(pauses)* So you think that I am under the influence of evil?

A: No ... well, actually, yes. Yes in the sense that we all are under the influence of evil in one way or the other. But the evil spirit is looking at every person's unique situation and is actively searching for a way to lead us astray. The good news is that God is actively trying to lead us back to himself. And I'd go so far as to say that we've just now discovered how God is doing that in your case. I dare say we've found the way to life.

M: Unbelievable ... it makes me think of the image of the angel on your right shoulder and the devil on your left.

A: Hmm. Do you think that what I said is far fetched? Or does it help you to understand what happened in this conversation?

Note how Pastor Anne is simply explaining what she's hearing. She introduces the concept of the discernment of spirits, albeit in a customised (and therefore incomplete) manner. Should she have explained things more fully? Or is it best to explain this bit by bit? You must always gauge this in the situation. Was I too extensive? Too restrained? Did I say something too early or too late? It's always a matter of trying one's best and of trial and error.

It is most important that you allow the directee enough space and time to process – and perhaps discard – the new information. The best thing for Pastor Anne to do is simply to continue the conversation for a bit. Recall that Margaret thought that she was under the influence of evil and that Pastor Anne was able to clear up this misunderstanding. Perhaps another example is necessary to help her understand this better? In any case, you can't simply ignore such misunderstandings without addressing them.

Moreover, note that your explanations of what you're hearing can treat other topics besides the discernment of spirits. For example, you could notice that someone has psychological issues and then suggest that he seeks professional help. You could also hear of someone's talents and gifts and then choose to reflect those back to him. Finally, sometimes you may also hear that someone has difficulty in addressing their rough edges and focus on that.

Explaining what you're hearing can greatly contribute to the directee's growth in spiritual maturity. By doing this, you provide the directee with vocabulary and a frame of reference – a legend, if it were – that equip him to better perceive and evaluate what is happening in the soul.

Making a Choice

When it comes to a person's growth in spiritual maturity, the ability to actually make a choice is also centrally important. Ultimately, spiritual maturity not only deals with gaining insights, learning vocabulary, or coming up with examples; it also has to do with what you actually do with those things. What really matters is whether the directee is able to live a better spiritual life after she has acquired better understandings, insights, and words to explain her spiritual experience.[61]

The example of Margaret can serve here as a good example. Imagine that Margaret is indeed helped by Pastor Anne's explanation. Imagine that afterwards, they have a good conversation so that Margaret clearly demonstrates that she understands what's at stake in her situation. In that case much ground has been gained – though there is still more progress to be made. Her insight must now become expressed in concrete, practical decisions; it must, in other words, 'take flesh' in Margaret's own life. If a spiritual director invites her directee to do this, that is also an example of formation – it helps the directee to take control of her spiritual life. In Margaret's case, the conversation could continue as follows:

> A: Margaret, might I suggest a further step for you to take? Earlier we talked about the two worlds and the difference

---

61 The things I discussed earlier pertaining to Ignatius' rules for discernment, namely, that they always should have a practical goal, are valid here as well. See Chapter 2 for further elucidation.

between them. Afterwards I suggested that this difference had something to do with God, and I asked if you agreed. We've already made quite the journey together. Yet I still think that we could, perhaps, go even further. (*pauses*) Is that ok? Or is it all enough already?

M: No, it's fine – go ahead.

A: Well, I actually wonder whether this whole experience can be understood quite practically as well. If it's really the case that the feelings of isolation, cold, and darkness have nothing to do with God while the feelings of life and light are from God, what does that mean? Could you do something as a result of this realisation? My own spiritual tradition teaches us that we can do something with that revelation. For example, if you know that the feelings of heaviness and darkness aren't constructive, you can give it very little attention. What do you think?

M: So you think that I should just ignore those cold and dark experiences? That I should not give much attention to it?

A: Yeah, actually, that's what I mean. Do you think that would work for you? Would you find that useful?

M: Hmm, well, maybe ... but isn't that kind of like burying my head in the sand?

This could once again be a moment for further clarification. Anne could explain the difference between the 'head in the sand' strategy and the (more subtle) approach of spiritual discernment. Spiritual discernment is not about ignoring what is going on but rather about highlighting the truth of God's light and minimising (rejecting?) the influence of evil.

Here too I would like to conclude with a couple of evaluative comments. First of all, this case is pretty straightforward; Margaret is a model directee: open, aware, and verbal. Not all directees are as expressive as Margaret. If your directee has difficulty in following you, or if she doesn't agree with the things you suggest, it's best to simply let it go. If you've said something useful and if your rapport is good, it will find a way to come back to the directee when the moment is right. It could also be an indication that you should leave some topics for your next conversation – you can't do everything all at once.

Moreover, this example was abundantly clear and a bit dramatic. Oftentimes the discernment of spirits is simpler and more modest. When someone says that she felt very content while on vacation, that a conversation with a certain someone was very useful, or that a new method of prayer was fruitful, this is enough for a deep conversation. In such cases, you can ask questions about what made the experience so positive and invite the directee to consider whether it has a concrete and practical meaning in her life. What path leading to life is revealed here? What is the choice that is being presented here?

Finally, as was also the case in the other formative interventions discussed, it's important to remain restrained. The core of spiritual direction is to talk about how God interacts with a particular person and, thus, about spiritual experiences. Teaching and forming are always secondary.

A warning given by Barry and Connolly, two experienced spiritual directors, may serve as an appropriate conclusion to this chapter. They warn particularly novice spiritual directors that the goal of spiritual direction is to help the directee discover the way God relates with him, and not to teach the Church's dogmas, theology, morals, etc.: 'Teaching, preaching, and moral guidance are not the proper task of spiritual directors. Their task is to help people experience God's action and respond to God. Fostering discovery rather than teaching doctrine is their purpose'.[62] This warning could equally be applied to everything included in this chapter under the heading of forming for spiritual maturity.

---

62 Barry, Connolly, *The Practice of Spiritual Direction*, p. 43.

9

VOCATIONAL SPIRITUAL DIRECTION

A special kind of spiritual direction is when you accompany people discerning a religious vocation. Perhaps you encounter a physical therapist who timidly admits to you that she sometimes has dreams of entering the convent. You may meet a biology major who tells you very convincingly that he wants to become a minister. Or you may find yourself directing someone who has begun to doubt her desire of being a high school religion teacher because the required studies intimidate her. It's not unusual for people discerning a vocation to be younger and therefore there is a great responsibility to guide them with care and wisdom.

In any such case, you can rely on the tools we've already discussed: taking it easy, listening attentively, focusing on where you sense movement, deepening, evaluating and discerning, and forming for spiritual maturity. However, it should also be stated that this is a unique kind of spiritual accompaniment. In this chapter, therefore, I'd like to dedicate some attention to the topic of vocation accompaniment.

For example, consider eighteen-year-old Elizabeth who has just returned from a pilgrimage to Taizé with members of her university parish. It was great! She really enjoyed the silence and stillness in the church, to the point that she would love to go and become a part of it by giving up her studies and becoming a monk in the Taizé community. That's impossible, of course, and she understands this herself. She wants to know if you are aware of a women's alternative to Taizé? She also has doubts about this, particularly as she has difficulty imagining giving up her family. Do you have some good advice for her?

The unique feature of this kind of spiritual direction should become immediately obvious: there is something very concrete at stake here. Up until this point, spiritual direction mainly treated general topics: prayer, reconciling with one's past, growing in connection with God. In this case, however, it treats a very concrete inquiry: 'What should I do? Can you help me?' In this chapter, I'd like to say a few things about a possible strategy to address these sorts of questions.[63]

Before we get started, let me clarify that a religious vocation does not necessarily relate to convents, ministry, or priesthood. A vocation is a calling to serve God and humanity in the broadest sense of the word; it is holistic and relates to professions, life projects, commitments, and relationships. I have decided to work in this chapter with the case of Elizabeth and to focus mainly on examples related to ministry for reasons of pedagogical clarity.

A Two-Phase Process

First of all, it's important to transform the solution-oriented 'what to do' conversation into a spiritual one. This pressing question which prompted the conversation should be delayed a bit. It is too early to give advice.[64] What deserves attention first is what is happening in the directee's soul and, ultimately, the way he or she relates to God. In other words, the

---

[63] Drawing on the *Spiritual Exercises*, Ignatian spirituality distinguishes three different ways of discerning life choices (see *Spiritual Exercises*, nos. 175–188). The first is through an experience of immediate clarity, such as the disciples of Jesus who 'immediately' left everything to follow him once they were called. The second is through engaging in the discernment of spirits wherein one attempts to sense what the good course of action should be. Finally, the third consists of a series of mental exercises wherein you attempt to make a reason-based decision; this can be a consideration of the pros and cons of a given decision or a consideration of how you would look back on a decision from your deathbed (or alternatives to that, such as imagining what a friend would counsel you). Experts often comment that the first manner should still be confirmed by the second. Moreover, the practices associated with the third method are often considered as a Plan B. In what follows I will speak of the second manner of discerning a decision, as it is the most common and useful one. For more on the uniqueness of this approach, see Moons, 'Pleidooi voor een alternatieve strategie bij pastorale dilemma's'.
For a more extensive treatment, see the enlightening book by Timothy Gallagher, *A Handbook for Spiritual Directors: An Ignatian Guide for Accompanying Discernment of God's Will* (New York: Crossroad, 2017). For my critique of Gallagher's approach, see Chapter 1.

[64] Cf. Barry and Connolly's sharp critique of the 'almost universal and deeply entrenched tendency of ministering people to want to inculcate truth, to teach, to instruct' that I quoted in Chapter 2 and the vision of accompaniment presented in that chapter.

spiritual director's job is to reorient the conversation.

I consider this a two-phase process. The spiritual director's first service is to facilitate a kind of initiation into the world of God and the soul, which we could call mystagogy. Only after you've done this do you come to the second phase. You then invite the directee to slowly and calmly return to the concrete question, to see what seems to be the better way of life in the light of the relationship with God that the directee has become more aware of.

This means that, while Elizabeth wants to know whether a women's alternative to the Taizé community exists, the spiritual director wants to find out what is going on within her soul. While she is focused on her dilemma of choosing between her family or a religious community, the spiritual director is interested in looking at what is going on below the surface.[65] Below I present a possible way to go about doing that:

SD: So it sounds like you had a really great experience in Taizé.

E: Yeah, it was amazing! And I totally wasn't expecting it.

SD: So you had a certain idea of what to expect, and the reality was far better?

E: Yeah. From the moment we entered Taizé, I could see that it was different. Everywhere I looked, I saw young people in cool clothes and no older people. And all of these young people were quiet. It was really, really quiet …

SD: So it was really quiet.

E: Yeah, totally. It was so calm. I really could feel it too, first all around me and then I felt it inside too.

SD: Ah, the silence made you feel calm.

E: Yes…it was almost as if I could hear the silence…first around me, then within me.

---

[65] Note that you should not immediately focus on the fact that it is not possible for a woman to join a male community or on the gender question. Recall what your job is: to be a spiritual director. Your job is not primarily to talk about rules and Church teaching.

SD: That's interesting. (*stresses the words*) *You could hear the silence.* What did you hear?

E: Hmm, yeah, I really don't know how I'd describe it. I mean ... it was just so different. I always listen to music: when I'm doing homework, when I'm jogging ... even in the bus on the way to Taizé. And then once we got there, there was nothing except silence. It was so weird ... yet also warm and comforting.

SD: Ah, ok. The silence was new, weird, and yet also comforting ... even warm.

E: Yeah, warm. It was almost as if the silence welcomed you home. A bit like when you're invited inside to a room with a roaring fire after you've been outside in the cold.

Notice how you consistently focuses on those words that suggest a spiritual dynamic. In order to increase the chances that Elizabeth allows herself to be led to her soul, you do this as gently as possible. This seems to be working too, because she goes from describing her experience as 'amazing' to it being like a 'warm and calm silence'.

You could also have chosen to pursue Elizabeth's use of the word 'inside'. Had you done that, the outcome would probably have been the same.

The underlying assumption of the two-phase method I'm proposing in this chapter is that God takes part in peoples' journeys, yet that we need time (and accompaniment) to get used to God's voice as it speaks in our souls.[66] Insofar as a vocation is a question of the soul (and thus of spiritual sensitivity), becoming accustomed to this voice has priority. Many things will appear to be happening which we might otherwise ignore. In Elizabeth's case, there is silence, calm, warmth, and welcome. Had you pursued the direction Elizabeth started out on, the conversation would have stayed on the level of the 'head' rather than that of the soul.

---

66 The various theological interpretations of the question if and how God 'speaks' to or calls someone is an important one, as is the question of the various interpretation of Divine Providence. As this is a book on accompaniment, I will however not delve into these questions here.

Elizabeth appears to be easily led to the domain of her soul. Up until this point, things are going quite well. It could also go less smoothly. For example, Elizabeth might not allow herself to be led to her soul. She might not be able to find her words or might be uncomfortable in exposing this side of herself. It could also be the case that things start out well and she appears to be going along with you, but then she suddenly stops and tries again to ask questions about her concrete dilemma. Finally, she may even actively protest: 'You're not taking my question seriously!'

Regardless of what happens, the best thing for you to do is to stay focused on the plan: you want to talk about her soul. Even though you are in no rush and are willing to be patient, that is where you hope Elizabeth will go. Sometimes it can be helpful to explain what you're trying to do and why (in the previous chapter I gave an example). In this case, you could proceed as follows:

SD: So Elizabeth, up until now we've been talking about your soul and the things that have been happening there. But you came to see me with a number of concrete questions about the existence of a women's Taizé community and about what life-choice you'd like to make.

E: Yeah I really struggle there ... We've really had a nice conversation ... but for heaven's sake, what should I do? I'm sorry to say it that way ... but I still don't know what I should do.

SD: (*Smiles*) And you'd really like to know that.

E: Yes, of course I'd like to know that!

SD: Ah, I see. (*Brief pause*) You know, Elizabeth, I hesitate to say this, but I propose that we actually delay addressing your question for a bit. It's September. Let's say that we revisit that question in January or so. Obviously, we're not going to forget your question, but first we're going to do something a bit different. Let's say that indeed God is calling you. Have you considered the way God actually speaks to you and what he's trying to tell you? Have you considered the way God looks at you? Have you ever enjoyed God's companionship? I have the impression that your experiences in Taizé are so rich. Let's unpack your experiences further: your experience of silence, of prayer. Would you mind if we worked with that first?

E: Ok, so you're saying that, for now, I shouldn't think about the future.

SD: Well, I mean, you can do whatever you like! You are the captain of the ship of your life! But I think that we don't need to get overly practical too quickly. Think of it like a house: first we pour the foundation, then we build the house.

E: I don't really understand that. What do you mean by 'foundation'? What is that?

SD: Your soul is the foundation. It's the power of attraction which you felt, the God who calls you ... The 'house', well, that's your concrete question. It's a two-phase process. In the first phase, we'll come to know God a bit better: how God interacts with you, and where he touches you and how. Only after we've considered these things will we address your concrete question in the second phase.

E: So what do I have to do? How does this two-phase process work?

SD: Well, first of all, I would propose that you to stop thinking in terms of what you 'have to' or 'must' do. As soon as you notice that you're drifting in the direction of thinking that way, it's better to try and avoid going there. Just gently wave goodbye to that feeling and let it pass you by. I would recommend that you devote some time and attention to prayer and spirituality instead. I think it

> would be a good idea if you commit to a daily practice of prayer or meditation, and in our conversations, we'll talk about how you're experiencing that.

In this case, Elizabeth allows herself to be won over relatively easily. Sometimes, however, it goes less smoothly. If so, you'll have to explain what you're doing, possibly in a couple of different ways. After that, then you begin with a sort of mystagogy: an initiation into the secret world of the soul.

Phase 1: Mystagogy

What I've been describing so far is in fact a form of mystagogy. That is what the first phase is about. Your goal here is to enable the directee to make contact with what is going on in his soul. This has to do with the importance of 'spiritual experience' (see Chapter 2) and, to put this in explicitly Christian and Ignatian terms, the importance of the Creator dealing directly with the creature. At this stage, the spiritual director has a similar role to that of a parent who is teaching her child to ride a bike. In that role, it does not matter so much what the parent is experiencing but, rather, what the child is experiencing. In other words, the focus is not on the (much needed!) knowledge and wisdom of the director but on the directee's own unique relationship with God.

The word mystagogy suggests someone being initiated into something. Indeed, for most directees, the world of the soul is fairly uncharted territory. Certainly, it is frequently true that someone has already had a powerful religious experience, as was the case with Elizabeth in Taizé. The soul has already given a clear sign of life to the directee. This sign is frequently the precipitating factor to the conversation about vocation that you're now having. With some help, Elizabeth will be able to provide more words to describe this experience. That is already a form of mystagogy, yet there is much more to the soul. Most of the time, it's difficult to identify one 'big' experience, and that is not a bad thing. Much more frequently the soul gives smaller signs of life instead: experiences and signs from everyday life. In order to discern a vocation, the directee has to make note of all of these signs, the big and small, and be able to map them out.

The director has two types of tools at his disposal to assist here. The first tool is to engage in conversations such as we've outlined in this book, including, of course, the example of Elizabeth we've just discussed. In order to do this, you will need a great deal of patience as you calmly and slowly go about your work.

The second tool you can use to initiate a directee into the world of the soul is to help her to pray. Formal prayers can really help here: the Our Father, Hail Mary, the Liturgy of the Hours, etc. It can also be useful to recommend that she visit churches, attend liturgies, and receive Holy Communion. Nevertheless, I'd like to advocate for a meditative form of prayer which is able to help the individual sit still with all of the things going on inside of her soul. Encourage the directee to pray, in other words, with the experiences she has undergone and with other spiritual experiences, no matter how modest. Here 'prayer' means: to note, to wonder, and to ponder.

Concretely, I will frequently invite directees considering a vocation to commit some time each evening to consider what happened to them during the course of their day (including but not limited to experiences of prayer). Where did they experience calm and disquiet? Where did they experience joy, happiness, faith, hope, and love, and where did they experience the opposite? And can they linger a bit on the inner movements, particularly, the good ones? Preferably, I encourage them to choose one of these movements, however small, and dwell on that one. Doing something like this every day gradually enables them to see what is happening in their soul. They learn to recognise and better appreciate it. Or, to put it into more explicitly 'religious' language: they become accustomed to God's inner consolations in the course of daily life.[67]

It helps if you're able to present this very concretely. Think with Elizabeth, for example, about the best way to become quiet and calm:

---

[67] This is a variant of what is called in Ignatian jargon the 'Examen Prayer'. For an extended presentation of this form of prayer along with detailed commentary, see Timothy Gallagher, *The Examen Prayer. Ignatian Wisdom for our Lives Today* (New York: Crossroad, 2006). For a creative presentation of variants on the Examen, see Mark Thibodeaux, *Reimagining the Ignatian Examen. Fresh Ways to Pray From Your Day* (Chicago: Loyola Press, 2015).

maybe laying on the bed, sitting comfortably in a chair, or going for a walk in a quiet street. Then help her determine how to begin, perhaps with a song or a short prayer. At this point, help her understand how to consider the events of her day and what stands out for her. Also make sure to tell her that she should try to focus on one particular thing and not to be overwhelmed by the number of things she has experienced during the course of her day. Finally, you'll want to tell her that this exercise doesn't need to last too long: it's better to commit to something short which can be easily done every day. A healthy realism almost always produces the best results. This could be done as follows:

SD: So what's a good way for you to do that, to calmly consider what's going on in your soul?

E: I think it would be good to try that in the evening.

SD: (*nods*) The evening is a good time for you.

E: Yeah, maybe before I go to bed?

SD: Ok. How would you go about doing it then? Would you go for a walk? Or do you have a comfy chair to sit in? What helps you become calm and quiet?

E: Hmm ... yeah, that's a good question! Well, I think it would be good if I take my shower first. That always helps me to relax at the end of the day. Then I'd make myself a cup of tea and light a candle. Would that be good?

SD: As long as those things help you relax, that's all that matters. (*pauses*) It sounds a bit like a ritual to me: shower, tea, candle ... And then you'd look back over your day?

E: Yeah. Though I'm not sure how I should actually do that. It's not as if I can remember everything ... so much happens over the course of a day.

SD: You don't have to remember everything. Even if you forget significant things, that's not really what matters. It's enough just to remember one good thing and to sit with it for a while.

Notice that you are doing a bit of formation here. You ask Elizabeth about a way to calm herself down at the end of the day and thereby put making a concrete plan on the agenda. You point out that all that matters is whether the method helps her to relax. You also point out that remembering one thing from the day is enough, rather than becoming overwhelmed at trying to remember everything. Ultimately this is about 'what helps Elizabeth find God', 'what helps Elizabeth connect to God's wavelength', yet in this case, the lighter, more implicit language seemed enough.

Note that this is formation in a low-threshold way: spiritual direction isn't a class or seminar (see Chapter 8). When you talk about this prayer practice, you should therefore be careful not to overwhelm your directee: don't try to do everything all at once. Initially, you can talk about the good things that happened in the course of the day. Later, you can be more precise: when did you feel close to God? When did you feel warmth and closeness? When did you feel most alive? What moments helped you to grow in faith?

Or, to explain this in another way: at first, it's more than enough to talk about 'being still' or 'calm' without immediately informing your directee why this is important. At this point you'll probably introduce words such *pondering*, *lingering*, *meditation*, and *contemplation*. You may also note to your directee that such experiences will become more tangible and more prominent as she pays attention to them. You should also advise against overthinking or theologising her experiences or making grand moralising statements such as, 'I'll be thankful for this experience from now on'. When someone gives you a bouquet of flowers, rather than analysing, you can simply accept and enjoy them.

In subsequent conversations, you should check in to see whether or not this method of prayer is working. Are the pancakes turning out, or are they burning, or worse yet, not cooking through at all? As soon as you sense that your directee has become comfortable with this form of prayer, then you don't need to discuss the method of his prayer any longer. This is certainly the case once the directee is able to talk about his prayer experiences and if there are fruits present. In such a case, the prayer 'works' – it has flavor – such that you can shift your focus to the content of the prayer.[68] In order to go about that, you can rely on the tools we've already talked about in the previous chapters: taking it easy, noticing where the water is bubbling, focusing to deepen, discerning, and finally, engaging in formation.

You only have to return to the directee's prayer practices if you notice you've exhausted the discussion of his experiences. Note, however, that this return to prayer practices should come about only when there is nothing to talk about more, not because of your directee's discomfort in talking about his soul (or due to your lack of ability to go deeper). Also note that sometimes spiritual experience is more present in daily life than in the prayer itself; that does not need to mean that the prayer is wrong. If the conversations run out of steam, it's indeed useful to return to the kind of prayer practices that he is engaging in, or simply discussing life in general. Perhaps a change of focus will then bear fruit and give you something more to talk about.

Finally, you should note that your conversations don't have to be overly long – even thirty minutes can suffice. Oftentimes you'll need to engage in some small talk in the beginning before you get down to business and start talking about what's going on in the directee's soul. Before bringing your conversation to a close, you may give a few specific instructions or recommendations. When you first start your sessions, you could see each other somewhat more frequently, perhaps once a week or every other week, so that you have a good chance to get things rolling in the right direction. Once things get going, you could shift to seeing each other once a month or every six weeks.

Intermezzo: Vocation as an Escape

Occasionally, as in the story of Samuel, vocational discernment happens upside down. Samuel thought he was hearing Eli calling out to him when it was actually God who was calling him. Similarly, sometimes people mistakenly think that God is calling them to marriage, celibacy,

---

68 In one of his instructions for spiritual directors, Ignatius says precisely the same thing but in reverse: if inner movements are lacking, then the director should ask what practices the directee is doing when engaging in prayer (see *Spiritual Exercises*, no. 6).

religious life, the priesthood, the permanent diaconate, or any other calling or ministry when in fact someone or something else is calling. It could also be the case that they are indeed hearing God, but God is actually telling them something other than what they initially thought.

A classic example is someone who has just converted to Christianity, who felt deeply moved by God to become a Christian and now wants to make an act of radical dedication. What better way to do this than deciding to devote one's life to ministry in the Church? This example shows how being authentically moved by God can be quickly mistranslated into a concrete plan of action. While there is little reason to doubt that God has moved this individual and has inspired him to dedicate his life to God, there is reason to doubt the conclusion. It seems rushed. Is this person aware that there are many other ways to dedicate oneself wholly to God, and have these been considered as possible callings too?

Another classic example is someone who is a bit socially awkward or on the spectrum. Perhaps someone has been wounded by a hard childhood or is plagued by uncertainty because she is not a good student. It can also be the case that a person exhibits symptoms of social awkwardness because he has never had an intimate relationship with another human being. In any case, if such an individual presents himself as a candidate for ministry, this should prompt you to pause. Social awkwardness or spectrum personalities are not *ipso facto* reasons that a vocation to ministry is impossible: remember that you don't know what's happening between the Creator and the creature. Rather, this is a prime example of how spirituality and psychology may interact with each other. It could be that in this case the normal human desire to come 'home' and belong is simply wearing a religious veneer. If that is so, you should affirm this human desire while constructively questioning its expression in this particular form.

Other classic examples include someone who is completely unhappy in his line of work and so seeks out meaning and significance elsewhere. One can think of an overworked lay minister or burned out religion teacher who wants to 'get away from it all' by joining a monastery. A more delicate example is someone who wants to go into ministry in order to escape or sublimate his or her sexuality.

In all of these examples, there may well be authentic spiritual movement, but there is uncertainty as to what exactly that movement is and especially as to whether this translates into a vocation to the ministry. Perhaps 'escaping' into ministry as I called it is not the best way to describe this. If the spiritual movement is authentic and true, it may be better to say that our interpretation needs purification – which it always does. In Ignatian jargon we speak of 'disordered attachments'. In the context of vocation discernment, one can in fact be attached to many other things than God, whether it's status, security, approval, or even one's scars. If these disordered attachments have a major voice in how we interpret our (spiritual) experiences, we need (to use more jargon) the grace of 'indifference' that is, to be free from attachments and able to simply choose the good.[69]

So what should you do if you notice indications of attachments or a lack of freedom? The first thing you should do is to acknowledge that there is a chance that your own listening may be in need of purification. You might think that someone's story is so lovely, so deeply religious, that his motives are completely free, yet you should not be enchanted. No one can fully live up to the radical ideal of being completely free, indifferent, and unattached. You must be on guard to hear intimations of impure motives. Conversely, you may find somebody's story so weird that you are not open any more to God who moves in mysterious ways. Likewise, in such a case, you are not free.

Secondly, you do not need to completely change your strategy. Your first job remains mystagogy. You're not a judge who has to weigh everything your directee says in the scales to pass judgment. Accompaniment is about helping the directee to get more familiar with the movements of the soul and the way that God interacts with him. If you suspect impure motives, you don't need to immediately begin

---

[69] Cf. the full title of the *Spiritual Exercises*: 'Spiritual exercises to overcome oneself and to order one's life, without reaching a decision without some disordered affection', no. 21. Cf. the translation by Joseph Munitiz and Philip Endean, 'Spiritual exercises having as their purpose the overcoming of self and the ordering of one's life on the basis of a decision made in freedom from any ill-ordered attachment', in *Personal Writings*, p. 289.

admonishing and warning your directee in order to unmask them. That would not work well anyway. It may prompt a defensive reaction and trigger an argument. So much for the directee's confidence in you! Most importantly, it would disrupt the mood you're trying to create, which is about the intimacy of the soul, not about arguments and who is right.

Ideally, it's enough simply to follow your tried and true method. This might unfold in various ways. Perhaps some very clear experiences of God come up. Of course, those should be acknowledged as something beautiful. Possibly, you also see that the directee is growing in faith, hope and love; her spiritual life clearly bears fruits. You also see that your directee is so joyful that it's infectious. In other words, all this suggests that the foundation is well in place and strong. But as soon as you move to talking about concrete things or concrete aspects, the clarity begins to waver. The directee still feels a sense of vocation, but things get less certain the more concrete you get. That is not a good sign.

For example, Elizabeth might still feel called to becoming a religious sister, but beyond that things are quite vague. When you ask her to tell you what most appealed to her in the Taizé experience, all she can say is 'everything' or 'just the whole experience'. If you try to ask her what was going through her mind, she also has difficulty in articulating it. She can only describe her experience in vague and general language. Or the biology student who is considering the priesthood does not manage to book a meeting with the rector of the seminary. This is indicative that something is not right.

Another scenario could be that God never gives clarity to someone: it's almost like God stays hidden in a dark cloud. The first phase of the discernment process does not really work. You can't even establish the foundation, let alone start building the house. Again, this is not a good sign. It could be an indication of psychological issues that need to be addressed first.

Thirdly, if you suspect that disordered attachments play a role in someone's desire to pursue a vocation, try thematising your directee's motives. You must start this in the gentlest way possible, as in the conversation that follows:

SD: Elizabeth, what strikes me most is that all you're bringing up are the advantages to entering a religious community. I don't hear any doubts or sadness in your voice about not being able to see your family so often, or having to give up your studies. It's almost like these things don't really matter to you.

E: Oh. So you're not really supportive then.

SD: No, it's not that. Whatever decision you end up making is not about me. All I'm pointing out is that I don't sense that you have any doubts or struggles with your decision – almost like you wouldn't be leaving anything behind that's important for you.

E: Well ... I guess I would be leaving a few things behind. But I'm sure it is going to be so wonderful in Taizé!

SD: You bring up some wonderful things, but also that you are leaving some things behind. Aren't they important? Your family, friends, studies ...

E: Good Lord, there you go again!

What you have been doing here is simply mirroring. You tell the directee what you notice and then gives the directee the chance to react. If the directee doesn't follow your lead, then you should repeat this and tell the directee that you really think these things are worth examining. That is what you have done above. Elizabeth is clearly uncomfortable with what you are trying to do. Her exclamation at the end is somewhat manipulative. Don't be fooled by this: stick to the plan. If Elizabeth continues to resist this movement, it's probably best for you to tell her why you think your observation matters and why you are questioning her.

In that explanation you should specify that what she thinks is God's call might not be. Here's an opportunity for formation. You should tell her that not everything that looks or sounds like God is actually God. This should be done with humility, however, acknowledging that you could be wrong. Remember that your goal is the directee's coming to insight, not proving that you are right. If you come on too strongly, your directee may (quite understandably) become defensive. In this case, you won't succeed in helping your directee.

Finally, it's important to comfort and encourage your directee, especially if his insight into areas of possible disordered attachment grows. Oftentimes this will result in the need to say goodbye to something. There's always a chance that the directee might become sad, or angry at God, the faith, or himself. Your best response in such cases is to acknowledge what remains: a sincere desire to serve God, the completely normal human desire to be at home somewhere, a struggle with wounds from the past, etc.

Phase 2: Embracing One's Vocation

So far I have focused on the first, mystagogical phase. How do you make the transition to the second phase? How can you get back to issue at stake, the vocation question? For this, let's look once more at the case of Elizabeth.

After you've met with her for a few weeks or months, let's imagine that you begin to note a peacefulness in Elizabeth's soul. You start to see that she finds her center and direction in an underlying connection with God, regardless of everything else that's going on in her life. She exhibits a healthy sense of freedom to choose the right path, whatever that may be. It is then – and only then – that you can return to her concrete and practical question. While you have tried your best to avoid that question until now, the moment has now arrived to reintroduce it. You could do this as follows:

> SD: Well Elizabeth, we've been journeying together a few months now. I recall that the first time we met you told me about your wonderful experience in Taizé. As time went on, you had other powerful experiences as well. Through it all, you've become more familiar with God and have learned how to better sense God's presence

> through experiences of consolation and communion. Is that pretty accurate?
>
> E: Yeah, I think that's well put. (*keeps silent for a moment*) You know, I'm really an extrovert. You've taught me how to become calm and quiet. It's almost like I've been initiated into a new inner world.
>
> SD: The inner world is pretty beautiful, isn't it?
>
> E: Yeah! I never would have thought that ...
>
> SD: When we started our meetings, you had a pressing question: 'What should I do?' Back then, I suggested that we should first become acquainted with this inner world before we addressed your question. What do you think? Are we ready to go there?
>
> E: (*smiles*) Oh yeah, my question! I almost forgot it, you know. I'm joking, of course! But you know ... that question doesn't seem so important anymore.
>
> SD: Not so important?
>
> E: I mean, back then I thought I needed to know right then and there what I should do. Now it's like: 'Hmm, that would be nice to know'. It's become less urgent. Crazy, no?
>
> SD: Crazy?
>
> E: Yeah, I mean at first it was *so* urgent ... now it just isn't.
>
> SD: So the question remains, but it feels different. How would you describe the difference?

While you were planning on thematising her vocation – note how gradually the director does that – you now receive an unexpected bonus. Your two-phase strategy, including delaying her urgent question, has delivered an important fruit: the tension that surrounded the initial question has disappeared. You could call this fruit 'freedom': her preoccupation and urgency have vanished, which enables Elizabeth to be open to hear God's voice (instead of her own fixation). This is a clear sign that Elizabeth is on the right path, and it also confirms that she's ready to proceed to the next phase. She can now ask her question from a place of restful consolation rather than from a place marked by stressful agitation. You might want to talk a little bit about this difference and also explain why you're pleased with this movement within her (cf. Chapter 8). In any case, you then should turn back to the question of vocation which Elizabeth had at the beginning:

SD: So maybe now that you've arrived at this place of peace, we can look again at the question of vocation? Would that be ok?

E: Yeah, I'm actually kinda curious now that I think of it. How will we tackle that? You weren't so crazy about diving deep in the question, if I recall correctly.

SD: (*smiles*) Yes, that's correct. Maybe a good place to start would be to occasionally consider this question in the course of your daily meditation. Just do what you usually do: get relaxed, look back at your day, and linger over an experience that sticks out. After you've done this, bring in your question. Then consider which alternative sits most comfortably with your soul, with your spiritual experiences. Where can you sense communion with God? Where is this communion enhanced and where is it less apparent? Just try to go with your intuition and resist the urge to overthink.

E: Alright, I'll try it!

SD: (*smiles*) Well, it's great that you're so open to trying. But what do you think? Do you think this is something you'd like to do?

E: I think so. It sounds a bit like what I do when I go to Starbucks. Before I order I have to sense what my body needs most. Do I want coffee or tea? Then, what kind of coffee or tea? I have to think about those things before I'm able to say what I want. I don't know ... maybe that's a silly example.

SD: (*laughs*) Personally I always go for coffee, but I get what you mean!

Note that things go smoothly. Elizabeth seems very much on the right track. But you'll only be sure of this when she shares how it has worked out for her the next time you meet. If something does not work, you'll have to adapt accordingly.

At this stage it's also important to encourage Elizabeth to gain more information about her potential choice. After all, you can only engage in good discernment if you know and can experience what the various options actually entail. For this reason, it would be advisable for Elizabeth to return to do some volunteer work at Taizé and also talk to one of the brothers about her possible vocation. Moreover, if someone has a very clear idea of their vocation, it's a good idea to invite him to take a good look at another option before coming to a decision. In Elizabeth's case, this is something you'd have to do in any case: after all, she can't join the community of brothers at Taizé. A possible idea would be to advise her to check out various religious communities' websites and Youtube channels or read some interviews in order to help determine what kind of religious life appeals to her most.

Here again, restraint is in order. You should calmly encourage her to gain some input from other sources while also encouraging her not to get too carried away with excitement or worked up with all the research. Slow and steady wins the race, so to speak.

The fruits yielded by this process should be discussed in the same manner as we've presented in the preceding chapters.

Concluding Remarks

Finally, I'd like to make a few comments on concluding a vocation discernment trajectory. First of all, this process must be limited in time. Oftentimes, a year is more than enough. Sometimes you may need a year and a half, but you should be careful not to go on much longer than that: this trajectory is not meant to last forever. You could actually consider it as a kind of project with a definite end-date. It's not healthy if the directee stays focused on one particular question for an indeterminate amount of time. You could also put this into more spiritual terms: an absence of clarity can itself be clarifying. This means, ultimately, that there is no clear 'yes' or 'no' to the directee's question. Perhaps someone is not yet ready to face a particular question, or the question itself is not a good one. In any case, it's abundantly clear that the question is not leading to clarity. In such cases it's better to put a stop to this particular trajectory of spiritual accompaniment.

Sometimes it can be confusing when there are clear signs of consolation but no clear indication of a vocation. Isn't it tormenting to think that God allows his presence to be felt without clearly indicating how someone should best respond to that presence in his life? In such cases, Ignatius' distinction between consolation and its concrete application into practice can be helpful. If someone is truly experiencing consolation and if there are apparent internal and/or external spiritual fruits, then there is no reason to doubt that it is, in fact, consolation. Nevertheless, one can still wonder if his interpretation of consolation is correct.

The classic example of this is someone who becomes a Christian (Anglican, Protestant, Roman Catholic or otherwise) and then immediately wishes to become a priest or pastor. Let's suppose that the movement which led this individual to coming to the faith is correct and pure. However, the translation of this into a desire to become a priest or pastor is, in all probability, a bit less straightforward. After all, one's zeal to serve God can just as well be lived out as a teacher, surgeon, or grocery store clerk. When you choose to end a vocational trajectory with someone without arriving at vocational clarity, it's probably good to remind your directee of this fact. She should still trust in the consolation that is being experienced; but she should remain open to the many different ways this can be practically expressed.

Finally, how should you conclude a case when someone's clarity has grown? Probably such cases will come to a natural end. You can help this along by slowly and carefully continuing to thematise the directee's question, basing this in the directee's deep connection with God. My experience is that the directee will then probably come up with a concrete plan or decision by himself. Your main role here is to manage the process, not the content. That is, you are to make sure that this discernment proceeds neither too quickly nor too slowly. For example, if a person decides to join a religious community and carries out that decision as soon as possible, you could ask him to sit with this decision for a couple of weeks before acting on it. Or if your directee tends rather to be slow, you could invite her to undertake small steps such as writing an application letter or informing friends or family of the decision that she is considering. You could also invite her to use this time as one of joy and gratitude for having determined her vocation and to share that joy with God. That is both a way of thanking God and of checking if the consolation will be durable.

This can also work in the opposite direction: if a person is not taking any steps to gain more information, to write an application letter, or to inform their family, you could invite them to do so. This kind of input is an occasion for further discernment. What kind of effect does it have on someone's soul to talk to his family about the plans being considered? For example, does Elizabeth remain cool and collected in the face of her family's possible criticism, or does her sense of calling come crashing down in the face of opposition? Does consolation remain, or has the experience dampened it? Or, what would happen if she writes a letter to a novice mistress of a particular congregation? Does this bring happiness and confirmation or the opposite? Here as always, the same rule applies: take it easy and go step by step. As soon as someone is ready to progress to the next step, you should certainly do so: just be aware of moving either too quickly or too slowly.

CONCLUSION

At the end of this guide to Ignatian Practice I would like to conclude by relativising everything that I have written above. As I have mentioned more than once: spiritual accompaniment is not linear. When someone shares bits of his or her story with you during spiritual accompaniment, you cannot simply apply a schema, utilising one tool after the other. On the contrary, conversations are unpredictable, going forwards and backwards, diving into the depths and back to the surface again. Therefore, the most important quality of a spiritual director is *not* to follow the 'handbook' precisely – rather the contrary. A spiritual director is not a machine, slavishly grinding gears. You are rather the keeper of a charism, a gift of the Holy Spirit. Often you make your choices intuitively. Often it is necessary to be creative. You must definitely know the handbook, and then you must definitely leave it behind.

If I reflect on my own spiritual accompaniment, I observe that I hardly follow a system. I try to sit quietly, with my full attention and heart focused on the other person. Most of the accompaniment carries on in its own way. Most of the time I sense 'automatically' where I have to go, what I should and shouldn't do. Sometimes I weigh up options and slow myself down, and sometimes I push myself to try something new. I am quite spontaneous. Sometimes I think out loud. Most of what I do is done intuitively. Admittedly, that intuition is shaped by the principles in this book of practice, and also by experience. At the moment, however, it is mainly intuition that directs me, or to use the language of faith, the Holy Spirit.

Yet I continue to believe in the usefulness of a book like this one.

Theology speaks of both grace and works. Whatever we are and do, is both given and the fruit of our toil. For the art of spiritual accompaniment, this means that one's intuition cannot operate without a framework, neither can charism. This book, with its focus on tools, is therefore a kind of de-mythologisation of spiritual accompaniment. It is not an elusive mysterious reality that is inaccessible to ordinary mortals except for when God bestows it as his gift. Rather, it has a practical-spiritual logic which expresses itself in the form of concrete tools. This de-mythologisation has the practical advantage that people can learn the art of spiritual direction. It makes the charism of accompaniment more accessible.

One could object in the case of complicated spiritual accompaniment. Shouldn't I have written more about that? Let's say that someone who has suffered from abuse in any form comes for spiritual direction. Someone who is stuck in cynicism. Someone who is considering changing their Church: from Roman Catholic to Protestant or from Protestant to Roman Catholic. Someone has lost faith in God and no longer believes. Someone hates their priest (or the pope). There would be a lot to say about these and other complicated cases. What do you do in those gritty, difficult cases? What is this book worth in real life?

Within the limited purpose of *The Art of Spiritual Direction*, perhaps two thoughts will suffice. First of all, long live (spiritual) common sense! You are a spiritual director, not God, not a psychologist, not a teddy bear or a lifebuoy. It is not your responsibility what people do. Just like parents, you are sometimes powerless. Sometimes you have to say that explicitly: 'My role is to listen to your soul and to help you discover God in it, not to convert you, not to heal you'.

Secondly, if you have set yourself (and the other!) that limit, I believe this 'guide to Ignatian practice' can be worthwhile, especially for complicated cases. Precisely because you may not know what to do and your intuition may be darkened, you return to the basics: taking it easy, listening by following, focusing on inner movements, deepening them, evaluating them, possibly forming a little bit on the way. Then you are using the manual not slavishly, but as it is meant to be used, as a help.

Finally, in the Church there are many services. The service of the liturgy, the service of the word, of practical organisation and administration, of welcome, of care for the sick, and of catechesis. Spiritual accompaniment is also one of those services. That relativises – once more! – this book: there is more to do in the Church than spiritual accompaniment. And at the same time, it shows the significance of what this book is about: spiritual accompaniment is one of the ways to build up the Kingdom.

I wish fellow spiritual directors much happiness in their important service of facilitating the encounter with God – the God who, according to Ignatian belief, longs to be 'in direct contact' with his people, and who works and lives in their souls.

WORD OF GRATITUDE

This book is some sort of miracle. Who could have imagined that I would become a spiritual director, let alone write a book about it? When I was a kid, I talked much more than I listened. Every so often, I was sent to the hallway because I spoke before it was my turn in class. In high school, I was studious, eagerly raising my hand to give the right answer. It took some time for me to discover that there is depth in remaining silent and listening, and to learn how to do that. Anke Bisschops, my (now emeritus) supervisor at Tilburg University, taught me the principles of conversation technique and encouraged me to pursue listening. The Jesuits introduced me to that other world, besides the world of doctrine and theology, of inner movements in the soul. Especially Jan van de Poll SJ, Benoît Stoffels SJ, Paul Nicholson SJ, and Nikolaas Sintobin SJ played an important role in this. Courses at the Jesuit Center for Spirituality St Beunos in Wales provided some professional training. In the background, my mother and her innate talent for listening continually served as an example.

Being asked to accompany others was another important element that contributed to the miracle of this book. This started during my early ministry as a diocesan parish priest in the Diocese of Rotterdam (2005–2009), prior to joining the Jesuits. When I was invited in 2011 to become the student chaplain at the Tilburg School of Catholic Theology and the Fontys University of Applied Sciences, I found myself seriously involved in accompaniment work. Many students and others trusted me with their stories. Slowly but surely, I started to feel at home in the world of the soul and to grow in reverence for God's mysterious dealings with people. Later I was asked to give workshops on spiritual accompaniment for groups in the Netherlands and Belgium. The miracle's completion came when Johanneke Bosman and Pieter de Boer of Berne Abbey Publishers proposed that I could pass on my experiences in the form of this book. I thank them for their trust (and patience). I owe Anke Bisschops and Nikolaas Sintobin for their constructive feedback. I also am indebted to Paul Nicholson and Donal Neary for their belief in the project of an English translation. I would like to thank Annie Bolger and Derrick Witherington for much appreciated assistance in realising the translation. Finally, for their financial support, I wish to thank the Tilburg School of Catholic Theology (Tilburg University) and a benefactor.

The greatest miracle however is not this book but the God whose presence and action I am privileged to witness in spiritual accompaniment. He is not a God of the past, but a God of this moment. People experience joy, peace, goodness, patience, strength and courage, and feel that in these experiences God allows himself to be found. He is near to people through his Spirit and alive in the depth of the human soul. It would fill me with deep thankfulness if this book facilitates deeper conversation about that God.

APPENDIX

In this book I have aimed at speaking about spiritual accompaniment in an accessible manner, yet sometimes I have not been able to avoid the use of a number of technical terms. To make up for that, I will here provide some clarification of the following expressions: discernment of spirits, Ignatian spirituality, Ignatius of Loyola, the Jesuits and the Spiritual Exercises.

The Discernment of Spirits

The discernment of spirits, or spiritual discernment, is a form of practical spiritual wisdom. It presupposes that a human being is moved and inhabited by both God / good and evil, and that evil can disguise itself in seemingly good appearances. This makes it crucial to discern with both great sensitivity and great sobriety what kind of inspiration is speaking or working in a given instance. For example, a housefather who has just become a Christian wants to pray for an hour every day. Because of work and children, he will probably not succeed, so he may end up frustrated about himself, his life, his family, and God. What started out as a plan to get closer to God has resulted in the opposite, so we can see that his good intention could well have been inspired by evil. No wonder that for the monastic tradition, moderation (including spiritual moderation) has always been an important virtue.

In the Ignatian vision of discernment, the emphasis is on interiority and on fruits. What is the 'aftertaste' of a certain inspiration, and what fruits does it yield? Ignatius' first conversion is often used as an example to illustrate how this works. Struck by a cannonball during an overconfident defense of a castle, Ignatius ended up on a sick bed. The passionate Spaniard daydreamed about chivalry: castles, damsels, victory, but also about following Christ. Both dreams were enchanting. Yet he noticed a difference: the first dream withered quickly while the second retained its flavor. Gradually he understood that God wanted to tell him something through what was going on in his soul. (The point of the story, by the way, is not that chivalry is superficial and holiness is noble, but that God speaks through the affective effect in the soul.) By the way, this was only the beginning; it took Ignatius years to recognise the subtlety that characterises true discernment and to become free from his radical tendencies.

Fellow Jesuit Nikolaas Sintobin describes this as 'living on the compass of joy'. Myself, I prefer the language of taste and aftertaste. In addition, note that fruits matter as well, as mentioned in Chapter 7. What tastes like joy and leads to joy suggests that something that is right. Something that has to do with faith, hope, love, a zest for life, mercy, meekness, strength, Christ, the Holy Spirit. These things point the way. And the opposite, such as cynicism, selfishness, despair, does so in a negative way. That kind of affective aftertaste or fruits must raise the alarm: this seems to be the wrong way.

For a both serious and funny introduction to the theme of the work of the various 'spirits' in us, see C.S. Lewis, *The Screwtape Letters: Letters from a Senior to a Junior Devil* (London: Collins, 2012); interestingly the word discernment is not mentioned in the book. Timothy Gallagher extensively explains and comments on the two series of 'Rules for Discernment' found in the *Spiritual Exercises*, including lots of examples and advice on how to best to respond to the 'spirits', see *The Discernments of Spirits. An Ignatian Guide for Everyday Living* (New York: Crossroad, 2005) and *Spiritual Consolation. An Ignatian Guide for Greater Discernment of Spirits* (New York: Crossroad, 2007).

Ignatian Spirituality

This term refers to the spirituality that draws inspiration from Ignatius of Loyola, and that is therefore called Ignatian. It is one of the many spiritualities represented in the Christian Church, next to (amongst others) Benedictine, Calvinistic, charismatic or Franciscan spirituality. Central beliefs of Ignatian spirituality are that God interacts directly and personally with each human being and that God does so especially by means of what in technical terms is called consolation: the experiences of God's closeness, stillness, depth, gentleness, life, strength and so on that confirm a person on the right path.

For more on these beliefs, see the core values discussed in Chapter 2. For background, see James Martin's accessible and comprehensive book, *The Jesuit Guide to (Almost) Everything. A Spirituality for Real Life* (New York: Harper One, 2010), or Jim Manney's recent, short and sweet lexicon: *Ignatian Spirituality A to Z* (Chicago: Loyola Press, 2017). The older book by former Jesuit David Lonsdale remains worthwhile: *Eyes to See, Ears to Hear. An Introduction to Ignatian Spirituality* (London: DLT, 1990). For details and depth, see *Diccionario de Espiritualidad Ignaciana*, eds. Javier Melloni a.o. (Bilbao – Santander: Mensajero, 2007). Cf. the letter by Karl Rahner to his fellow Jesuits in which he adopted the persona of Ignatius, *Ignatius of Loyola Speaks*, tr. A.S. Kidder (South Bend, IN: St. Augustine, 2013); originally in German, '*Das Alte neu sagen. Eine fiktive Rede des Ignatius von Loyola an einen Jesuiten von heute*' (1978). For practicing Ignatian spirituality, see the daily accompanied meditations on the website and app Pray As You Go.

Ignatius of Loyola

Ignatius of Loyola was a Basque nobleman, born in 1491, who with a group of friends founded the Society of Jesus. At home in the circles of the court and a lover of worldly things, he suffered a dramatic hit by a cannonball while he was leading the defense of the city of Pamplona. The physical damage (he had a limp for the rest of his life) weighed heavily on him, especially because of his self-confessed vanity. On his sickbed, the courtier experienced a profound conversion: he would follow the Lord. At first, he did so in a literal sense, by pilgrimaging to Jerusalem. Forced to return to Spain, he engaged in spiritual conversations with people while also attempting to study theology, but again and again he ran into problems with the Inquisition. He continued his studies in Paris, where he shared a room with Pierre Favre and Francis Xavier. He convinced both men to join him in pursuing his ideal. In a chapel in Paris in 1534, they vowed together with a few others to stay together and serve God. In the last years of his life, Ignatius served as the Superior General (or 'Father General'), governing the tremendously growing Order; at his death in 1556, the Jesuits counted some thousand members. This growth came with major changes in the original ideal. For example, where Ignatius had initially thought of a small group of Jesuit pilgrims, requests for erecting schools let him to seriously commit the order to education, which led to a much more settled existence.

Solicited by his confreres, Ignatius dictated at the end of his life a spiritual autobiography: *Reminiscences or Autobiography of Ignatius Loyola, as heard and written down by Luis Gonçalves Da Câmara*. It is also called *A Pilgrim's Journey*, as he consistently spoke of himself as pilgrim. The story – which is selective and constructed, meant for formation rather than as a historical account – shows us a man who went through several conversions. Because of his passionate disposition, he initially exaggerated his zeal, for example by not eating or drinking for days at a time. Gradually learning moderation, he became familiar with the delicacy and subtlety that is the hallmark of true discernment of spirits*. This learning process was both a mediated and mystical event. Wise people around him played an important role and at the same time Ignatius clearly had mystical gifts by means of which God himself guided him.

In recent decades the representation of Ignatius has undergone major changes. From a spiritual 'Superman' and strict but fair Superior General, he came to be seen as a charismatic, warm-hearted man with a deep spiritual sensitivity. Although Ignatius undeniably had severe and sharp edges, the sources support this development. Yet like most people, Ignatius cannot be captured in only two portraits, all the more so because of his eventful and varied life. Jim Manney, for example, characterises Ignatius as a nobleman, soldier, pilgrim, student, friend, and superior general.

For a personal testimony of the shifting image of Ignatius, see Ron Darwen, 'Will the Real Ignatius Please Stand Up?', at www.thinkingfaith.org (30-7-2008). For an extensive introduction into Ignatius and the first Jesuits, see John O'Malley, *The First Jesuits* (Cambridge: Harvard University Press, 1993). For a very short introduction, see Jim Manney, *Ignatian Spirituality A to Z* (Chicago: Loyola Press, 2017).

The Jesuits

Appendix

The Jesuits are a group of Roman Catholic male religious, mainly priests, that was founded by Ignatius of Loyola and a group of friends. Just like the Benedictines, the Franciscans or the Dominicans (and their female variants), the Jesuits have their own strengths and peculiarities (not to mention weaknesses). Highly characteristic for the Jesuits is, for example, the discernment of spirits. Moreover, Jesuits often typically work in ministries other than parishes. Traditionally, they are involved in education and spiritual work, art and culture, theology and science (for instance, at the Gregorian University in Rome and at the Vatican Observatory).

Famous moments in the history of the Jesuits include firstly, the attempt by Matteo Ricci and other missionaries to preach the gospel with respect for the local culture, which led to the so-called Chinese Rites Controversy. According to the contemporary Roman Catholic philosopher Charles Taylor, this mirrors our own experience, for we too are faced with the difficult question what in culture contributes to faith and what hinders it.[70] Secondly, the young Society of Jesus stood out for its commitment to the indigenous peoples of South America. They were brought together into so-called 'reductions' to be safe from the Spanish and Portuguese slave hunters, as was dramatically depicted in the movie *The Mission* (1986). Thirdly, the Jesuits were marked by the shocking papal 'Suppression' of the order in 1773, yet to be restored in 1814. A final major moment has to do with the growing awareness in the years following the Second Vatican Council (1962-1965) that the Jesuit mission is about both faith and social justice; the slogan 'a faith that does justice' became programmatic.

The official name of the Jesuits is 'the Society of Jesus' or, in Latin, the *Societas Jesu*; that is why Jesuits may put SJ after their name. There are no female Jesuits, but there are numerous female congregations with Ignatian inspiration, such as the CJ Sisters (Congregation of Jesus), the Loreto Sisters (with IBMV after their name) who were founded in the

[70] See *A Catholic Modernity. Charles Taylor's Marianist Award Lecture*, ed. James L. Heft (Oxford: Oxford University Press, 1999). The lecture series dates back to 1996. According to Tayler, 'we are challenged to a difficult discernment, trying to see what in modern culture reflects its furthering of the gospel, and what its refusal of the transcendent. The point of my [Matteo] Ricci image is that this is not easy', p. 36. The pioneering Jesuit Matteo Ricci (1552–1610) played an important role in this Controversy.

seventeenth century by Mary Ward, and the *Soeurs de Saint André* who work (amongst others) in Taizé, France.

For accessible introductions, see John O'Malley, *The Jesuits: A History from Ignatius to the Present* (Lanham: Rowman & Littlefield, 2014) and Nikolaas Sintobin, *Jesuits Telling Jokes. A (Serious) Introduction to Ignatian Spirituality* (Chicago: Loyola Press, 2016) (originally in Dutch, 2013). Also recommended are the movie *The Mission* (1986) and Shusaku Endo's novel *Silence* (originally in Japanese, 1966) which was made into a movie by Martin Scorsese in 2016.

The Spiritual Exercises

The concept of 'the spiritual exercises' has various, overlapping meanings. Usually, the term designates a thirty-day retreat during which the retreatant engages with a set of topics, according to a specific method. In colloquial usage, this is called 'the thirty days'. Jesuits and other Ignatian religious do such a retreat as part of their novitiate training, yet it is open to lay people as well. The booklet in which these topics and this method are described is also called the *Spiritual Exercises*. This booklet is certainly not spiritual literature as, for example, the books of Henri Nouwen are. It is meant for the spiritual director, not the directee. Thirdly, the word is used to refer to adapted forms of the thirty-day retreat, for example retreats of five or eight days. And finally, according to Ignatius, the word can be used for all forms of reflection and prayer. As he writes in the sobering first Annotation in the *Spiritual Exercises*:

> By the term spiritual exercises, we mean every method of examination of conscience, meditation, contemplation, vocal or mental prayer, and other spiritual activities, such as will be mentioned later. For, just as taking a walk, traveling on foot, and running are physical exercises, so is the name of the spiritual exercises given to any means of preparing and disposing our soul to rid itself of all its disordered affections and then, after their

removal, of seeking and finding God's will in the ordering of our life for the salvation of our soul. (SE, no. 1)

As an aside, Ignatius did not invent the idea of spiritual exercises in general. Such exercises were common in the spiritual circles in which Ignatius moved and in which he learned to find his way in his soul and in prayer.

BIBLIOGRAPHY

Ignatian Primary Sources

Favre, Pierre. *The Spiritual Writings of Pierre Favre. The Memoriale and Selected Letters and Instructions* (St. Louis: The Institute of Jesuit Sources, 1996).
Ignatius of Loyola. The *Spiritual Exercises of Saint Ignatius. A Translation and Commentary by George E. Ganss* (St. Louis: The Institute of Jesuit Sources, 1992).
– *Personal Writings. Reminiscences, Spiritual Diary, Select Letters, Including the Text of the Spiritual Exercises*, tr. and intr. J.A. Munitiz and Ph. Endean (London: Penguin Books, 1996).
– *Letters and Instructions*, ed. and tr. M. Palmer, J. Padberg, J. McCarthy (St. Louis: The institute of Jesuit Sources, 2006).
– *Ignatius in zijn brieven. Vertaald en toegelicht door Mark Rotsaert* (Averbode: Altiora, 2015).
Institutum Historicum Societatis Iesu. *Monumenta Historica Societatis Iesu* (MHSI), *Monumenta Ignatiana Series Prima*, available online at http://www.sjweb.info/arsi/Monumenta.cfm.

Other Sources

Bakker, Bert. *Luisteren 2.0. Anderen tevoorschijn luisteren* (Gorinchem: Ekklesia, 2013).
Barry, William A., and William J. Connolly. *The Practice of Spiritual Direction*, 2nd rev. ed. (New York: Harper Collins, 2009), originally from 1982.
Buber, Martin. *I and Thou*, tr. R.G. Smith (Edinburgh: Clark, 1984); originally in German, *Ich und Du* (1923).
Darwen, Ron. 'Will the Real Ignatius Please Stand Up?', at www.thinkingfaith.org (30-7-2008).
Decrees of the Ecumenical Councils, ed. Norman Tanner (Washington: Georgetown University Press, 1990).
Diccionario de Espiritualidad Ignaciana, eds. Javier Melloni a.o. (Bilbao – Santander: Mensajero, 2007).
Pope Francis, *Amoris Laetitia. Post-Synodal Apostolic Exhortation on Love in the Family* (Vatican: Vatican Press, 2016), available online at vatican.va.
Gallagher, Timothy. *The Discernments of Spirits. An Ignatian Guide for Everyday Living* (New York: Crossroad, 2005).
– *The Examen Prayer. Ignatian Wisdom for Our Lives Today* (New York: Crossroad, 2006).
– *Spiritual Consolation. An Ignatian Guide for Greater Discernment of Spirits* (New York: Crossroad, 2007).
– *A Handbook for Spiritual Directors: An Ignatian Guide for Accompanying Discernment of God's Will* (New York: Crossroad, 2017).
Grün, Anselm, and Meinrad Dufner. *Spiritualität von Unten* (Münsterschwarzach: Vier Türme Verlag, 1994). Spanish translation: *Una espiritualidad desde abajo. El diálogo con Dios desde el fondo de la persona* (Madrid: Narcea, 2000).
Holgate, Ruth. 'Training Spiritual Directors', in *The Way. A Review of Christian Spirituality Published by the British Jesuits* 53/4 (2014), pp. 68–78.

Hughes, Gerard W.. *God of Surprises* (London: DLT, 1985).

Lewis, C. S.. *The Screwtape Letters: Letters from a Senior to a Junior Devil* (London: Collins, 2012).

Lonsdale, David. *Eyes to See, Ears to Hear. An Introduction to Ignatian Spirituality* (London: DLT, 1990).

Louf, André. *Grace Can Do More. Spiritual Accompaniment and Spiritual Growth* (Kalamazoo: Cistercian Publications, 2002); originally in French: *La grace peut advantage. L'accompagnement spirituel* (1992).

Bibliography

Malloy, Richard G.. *Spiritual Direction. A Beginner's Guide* (Maryknoll: Orbis, 2017).

Manney, Jim. *Ignatian Spirituality A to Z* (Chicago: Loyola Press, 2017).

Martin, James. *The Jesuit Guide to (Almost) Everything. A Spirituality for Real Life* (New York: Harper One, 2010).

Marsh, Rob. 'Receiving and Rejecting. On Finding a Way in Spiritual Direction', in *The Way. A Review of Christian Spirituality published by the British Jesuits* 45/1 (2006), pp. 7–21.

Moons, Jos, 'Affectieve orthodoxie', at www.igniswebmagazine.nl (2-2-2015).

– 'Onderscheid leren maken. Het noviciaat als casus', in *Cardoner. Tijdschrift voor ignatiaanse spiritualiteit* 32/3 (2013), pp. 28–35.

– 'Remembering as a Crucial Spiritual Tool. Pierre Favre's Spiritual Life according to the Memoriale', in *The Way. A Review of Christian Spirituality Published by the British Jesuits* 55/2 (2016), pp. 71–81.

– 'Help me onderscheiden. Ik heb een roeping', at www.igniswebmagazine.nl (26-2-2018).

– 'De erfenis van Ignatius. Onderscheiding als sleutel tot paus Franciscus', in *Katholiek Nieuwsblad* (29-7-2016), p. 10.

– 'Pleidooi voor een alternatieve strategie bij pastorale dilemma's. «Dat wij zouden aanvoelen wat Gods meest heilige wil is, en hem volbrengen» (Ignatius)', in *Internationaal Katholiek Tijdschrift Communio* 42 (2017), pp. 479-488.

– 'Rustig je roeping vinden. Drie handvaten voor begeleiders', in *Katholiek nieuwsblad* (22-6-2018), p. 14.

– 'Tijd maken voor het echte verhaal: God als troost?', in J. van der Vloet, I. Cornu (red.), *Overleven na de dood* (Antwerpen: Halewijn, 2018), pp. 27–29.

– 'Wat de studentenpastor doet? Zo weinig mogelijk...', at www.igniswebmagazine.nl (26-10-2017).

Nouwen, Henri. *Spiritual Direction. Wisdom for the Long Walk of Faith* (New York: Harper One, 2006).

Olivera, Bernardo. *Light for My Path. Spiritual Accompaniment* (Collegeville: Liturgical Press, 2009); originally in Spanish, *Luz para mis pasos. Iniciación al acompañamiento espiritual en contexto monástico* (2006).

O'Leary, Brian. *Pierre Favre and Discernment. The Discernment of Spirits in the Memoriale of Blessed Peter Favre*, 2nd rev. ed. (Oxford: Way Publications, 2006).

O'Malley, John. *The First Jesuits* (Cambridge: Harvard University Press, 1993).

– *The Jesuits: A History from Ignatius to the Present* (Lanham: Rowman & Littlefield, 2014).

Rahner, Karl. 'Christian Living Today and Formerly', *Theological Investigations*, vol. 7 (London: DLT), pp. 3-24; this is a substantially adapted translation on the basis of the original German, 'Frömmigkeit früher und heute' (1966).

– *Ignatius of Loyola Speaks*, tr. A.S. Kidder (South Bend, IN: St. Augustine, 2013); originally in German, 'Das Alte neu sagen. Eine fiktive Rede des Ignatius von Loyola an einen Jesuiten von heute' (1978).

– *Spiritual Writings*, ed. and intr. Ph. Endean (Maryknoll: Orbis, 2004).

Ruffing, Janet. *Spiritual Direction. Beyond the Beginnings* (New York: Paulist Press, 2000).

Sintobin, Nikolaas. *Jesuits Telling Jokes. A (Serious) Introduction to Ignatian Spirituality* (Chicago: Loyola Press, 2016).

– *Leven met Ignatius. Op het kompas van de vreugde* (Zoetermeer: Meinema, 2015).

van Steenbergen, Felix. 'De geestelijke begeleiding', *Collationes. Vlaams tijdschrift voor theologie en pastoraal* 27 (1997), pp. 393–408.

Taylor, Charles. *A Catholic Modernity. Charles Taylor's Marianist Award Lecture*, ed. James L. Heft (Oxford: Oxford University Press, 1999).

Thibodeaux, Mark. *Reimagining the Ignatian Examen. Fresh Ways to Pray from Your Day* (Chicago: Loyola Press, 2015).